Speed, Accuracy & Technique

for Guitar

Written by Greg Studley

COMPLETE GUIDE

All text and music exercises composed by Greg Studley.
Cover design and interior book design by Kim Wylie.

Published by Greg Studley.

ISBN 978-0-9899798-3-2

ACKNOWLEDGEMENTS

First and foremost, I would like to thank my family and friends for all of their support over the years. I am especially grateful to my best friend and partner in life, Tiffany, for her immense patience and honest opinions while composing the text and music for this book. A non-musician should never be subjected to listening to this many musical exercises.

Thank you to all of the great musicians and instructors that I have had the pleasure of crossing paths with over the years. You have all made me into a better musician and pushed me to always play my best.

To all of my students past and present, I would not have realized the value of these books if you had not walked into my studio and asked for me to show you how to become better players. It is all of you who have helped me to become a better music instructor.

INTRODUCTION

This book series is designed to gradually enhance three essential components of the modern guitarist – speed, accuracy and technique. Regardless of the musical genre that you are exploring, whether it be jazz, blues, rock, metal, country or otherwise, these three categories should all be in harmony to allow you to play your best. The exercises contained within this series will not only train the fingers of your fretting hand, but will also enhance your picking techniques and create synonymous movement between the two.

SPEED

The ability to play fast will enable you to add energy and excitement to your music. The exercises in this book will gradually become faster, increasing your ability to quickly move your fingers in different patterns. Many players can already move their fingers quite fast, but lack clarity in their playing. This is why speed must be accompanied by accuracy.

ACCURACY

One of the most difficult components to master is accuaracy. Every note should be clearly audible and each finger should react as desired to play any particular note. Training the fingers to do this is a task that requires much patience and often very slow playing at first. Throughout this series, numerous finger patterns are given to achieve a high level of accuracy when moving across the strings, transferring to adjacent strings, or skipping over strings.

TECHNIQUE

The most versatile players have a large array of techniques that they use to create a unique and professional sound. The most common of these techniques include slides, hammer-ons, and pull-offs. The goal of these exercises is to train the fretting hand to easily use these techniques at different speeds and between different fingers. To ensure accurate picking, the appropriate pattern of downstrokes and upstrokes will always be notated.

HOW TO USE THIS BOOK

This book should be used as a supplement to your everyday practicing. For best results, start off any practice session or performance preparation by playing an exercise for 5-10 minutes to coordinate your fingers and picking. Use a metronome to ensure that you are playing evenly, and are working towards playing each exercise at full tempo. If you are unable to play an exercise at its full tempo, play slowly and evenly to gradually increase your coordination. Keep track of your progress by writing the date of completion at the bottom of each page.

MUSIC NOTATION LEGEND

QUARTER NOTES

In standard music notation, a *note* is used to represent a tone, and the duration of that note is determined by its *value*. One of the most fundamental note values in music is the quarter note.

Quarter notes are represented as

MEASURES

Measures are groups of notes enclosed by vertical bar lines that are used to separate music into sections of equal value. These divisions are determined by the *meter*, or number of beats per measure. A *beat* is considered to be a strong pulsation of sound that is often constant throughout a piece of music. Modern music will commonly have either two, three, or four beats per measure.

TIME SIGNATURES

The *time signature* of a song, represented by two vertically-stacked numbers, will determine both the meter and the value that will define the beat. The top number designates the meter while the bottom number designates the value of the beat. Time signatures will always be found at the beginning of a piece of music. Here are some of the most commonly used time signatures:

2 Two beats per measure.
4 Each beat is a quarter value.

3 Three beats per measure.
4 Each beat is a quarter value.

4 Four beats per measure.
4 Each beat is a quarter value.

TEMPO

The speed of the beat for any musical piece is determined by its *tempo*, which is represented by a number. This number is a description of beats per minute (bpm). All exercises throughout this book will include a specific tempo for which they should be accurately played. These tempos will be notated above the first measure of the piece. It is highly recommended that you use a metronome to play each exercise at its notated tempo.

MUSIC NOTATION LEGEND

STANDARD NOTATION & TABLATURE

All exercises in this book will be notated with standard treble clef notation (notes located on a music staff with rhythmic values) and Tablature (TAB). The notes will define the rhythm that should be played, while the TAB will explain which strings and frets should be played.

HAND POSITIONS

It is important to know how to describe your *hand position* on the neck of the guitar. Your hand position is a description of what fret should be played by the first (index) finger of your fretting hand. Your other three fingers should be assigned to the next three frets. Hand positions are notated in the form of roman numerals underneath the music staff, above the TAB. Because TAB notates which fret to play on a string but not which finger to use, this is a very helpful way to describe which fingering should be used, while avoiding modern numbers that may become confusing next to the TAB.

ROMAN NUMERALS	I	II	III	IV	V	VI	VII	VIII	IX	X
MODERN NUMBERS	1	2	3	4	5	6	7	8	9	10

PICKING NOTATION

All exercises will have specific instructions on the best method of picking, which will be notated as downstrokes (⊓) or upstrokes (V) above the TAB.

SAMPLE MUSIC:

(time signature)

♩ = 60 *(tempo)*

III *(hand in 3rd position)*

(pick downstrokes)

3 4 5 6 | 3 4 5 6 | 3 4 5 6 | 3 4 5 6 | 3 4 5 6 | 3 4 5 6

fret 3 *fret 4* *fret 5* *fret 6*

(notes on 6th string) *(notes on 5th string)* *(notes on 4th string)* *(notes on 3rd string)* *(notes on 2nd string)* *(notes on 1st string)*

LEVEL 1: EXERCISE 1

To prepare yourself for all exercises to follow, you should first gain accurate control of your picking hand when playing quarter notes. Starting on the low E-string and using only downstrokes (⊓), pick four times on each string of the guitar, ensuring that you are playing exactly on the beat. This exercise may be played in repetition by playing from the last measure to the first measure without a break.

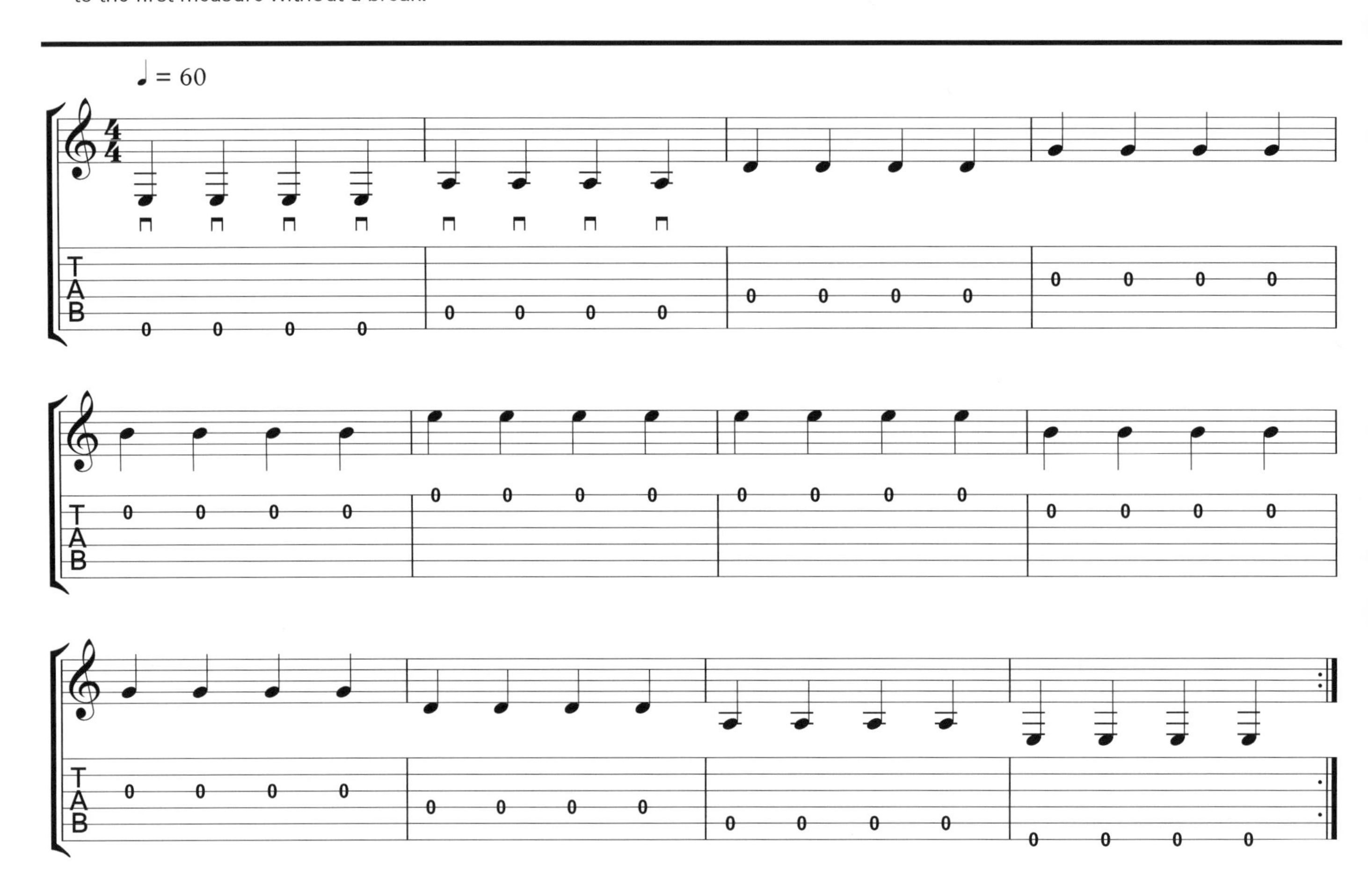

DATE OF COMPLETION: ______________________

LEVEL 1: EXERCISE 2

Starting on the low E-string and using only downstrokes, play the finger patter 1-2-3-4 on each string while keeping your hand in first position (notated as "I" above the TAB) and using one finger for each fret. Upon completing the pattern in first position, move up one fret to second position (notated "II") and play the reverse finger pattern (4-3-2-1) on each string, starting from the high E-string. For best sound and optimal technique, be sure to use your fingertips and place them at the end of the frets. Try to play legato, connecting all notes together with no gaps of sound. This exercise may be played up the entire length of the guitar neck.

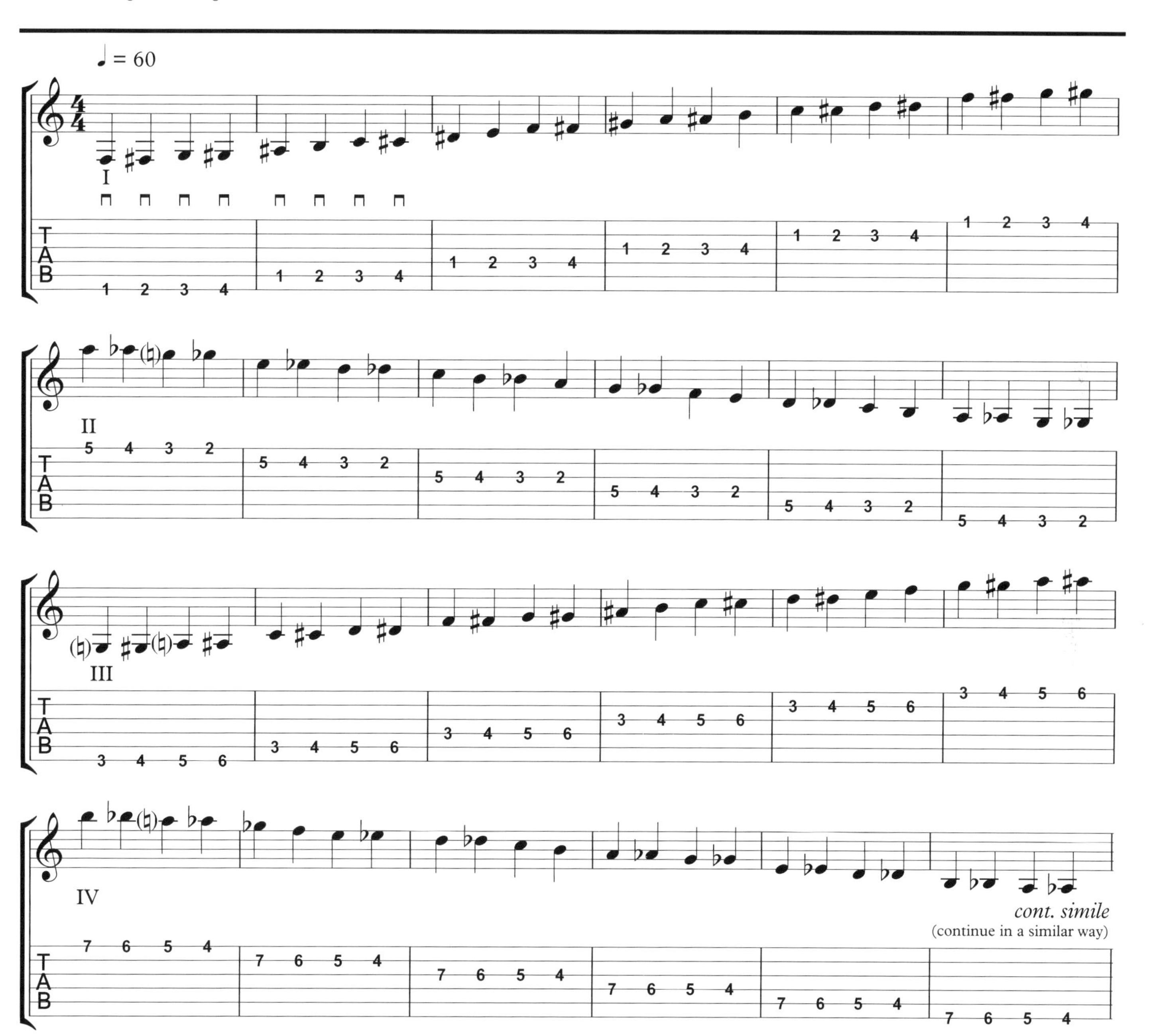

DATE OF COMPLETION: ______________________

LEVEL 1: EXERCISE 3

Starting on the low E-string and using only downstrokes, play the finger pattern 4-3-2-1 on each string while keeping your hand in first position and using one finger for each fret. Upon completing the pattern in first position, move up one fret to second position and play the reverse finger pattern (1-2-3-4) on each string, starting from the high E-string. Continue to use your fingertips and place them at the end of the frets. Try to play legato, connecting all notes together with no gaps of sound. This exercise may be played up the entire length of the guitar neck.

DATE OF COMPLETION: ______________________

LEVEL 1: EXERCISE 4

Starting on the low E-string and using only downstrokes, play the finger pattern 1-3-2-4 on each string while keeping your hand in first position. Upon completing the pattern in first position, move up to second position and play the reverse finger pattern (4-2-3-1) on each string, starting from the high E-string. This exercise may be played up the entire length of the guitar neck.

DATE OF COMPLETION: ____________________

LEVEL 1: EXERCISE 5

Starting on the low E-string and using only downstrokes, play the finger pattern 4-2-3-1 on each string while keeping your hand in first position. Upon completing the pattern in first position, move up to second position and play the reverse finger pattern (1-3-2-4) on each string, starting from the high E-string. This exercise may be played up the entire length of the guitar neck.

DATE OF COMPLETION: ______________________

LEVEL 1: EXERCISE 6

Using only downstrokes, play the finger pattern 1-2-3-4 while switching strings mid-measure (on beat 3). Upon completing the pattern in first position, move up to second position and play the reverse finger pattern from the high E-string, continuing to switch strings mid-measure. This exercise may be played up the entire length of the neck.

DATE OF COMPLETION: ______________________________

LEVEL 1: EXERCISE 7

Using only downstrokes, play the finger pattern 1-3-2-4 while switching strings mid-measure. Upon completing the pattern in first position, move up to second position and play the reverse finger pattern from the high E-string, continuing to switch strings mid-measure. This exercise may be played up the entire length of the neck.

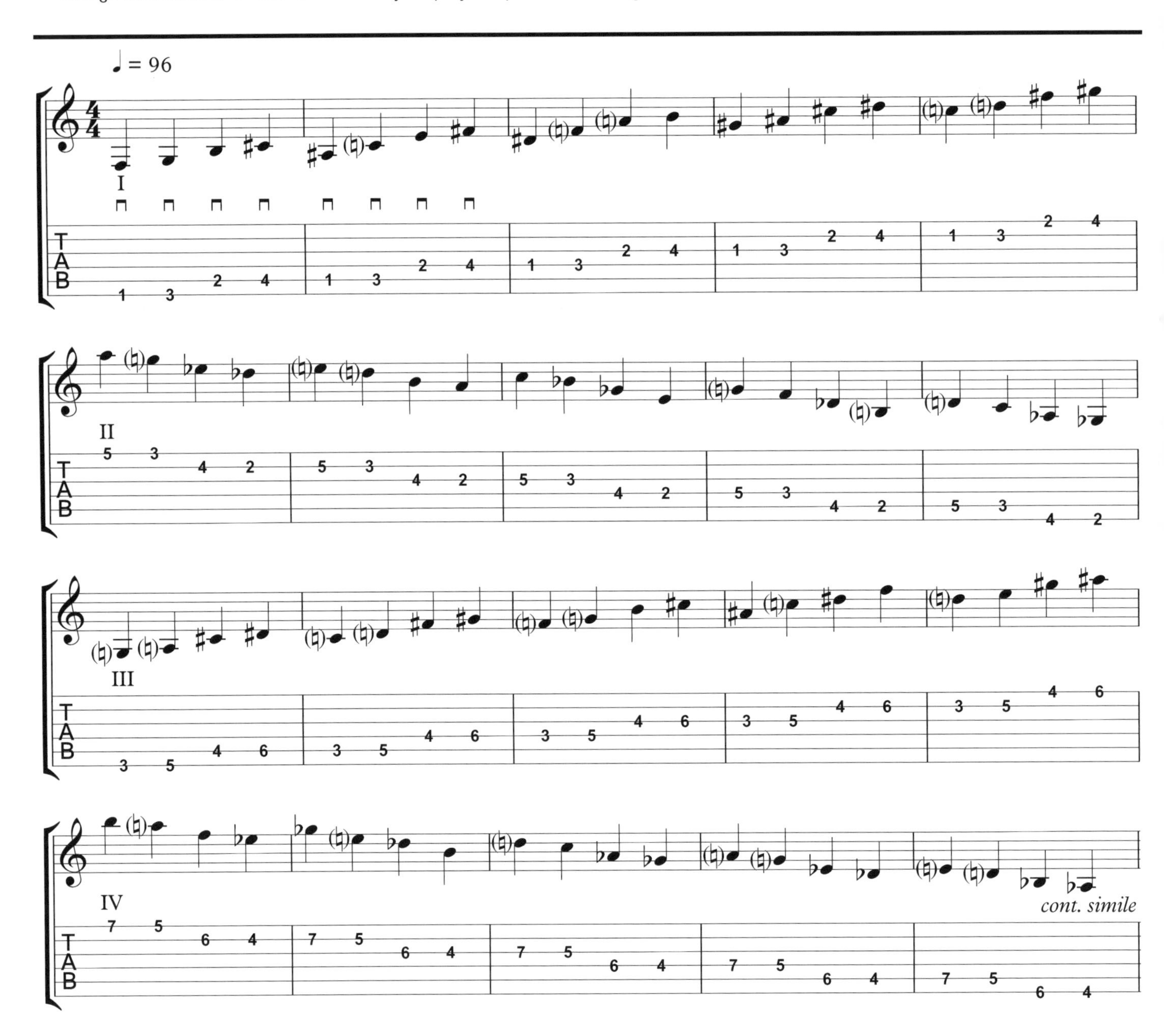

DATE OF COMPLETION: ______________________________

LEVEL 1: EXERCISE 8

This exercise will train each finger to "roll" from one string to the same fret of the next highest string. Be sure to play each initial note with your fingertip and then roll (or flatten) your finger onto the next highest string. Try to play legato, connecting all notes together with no gaps of sound.

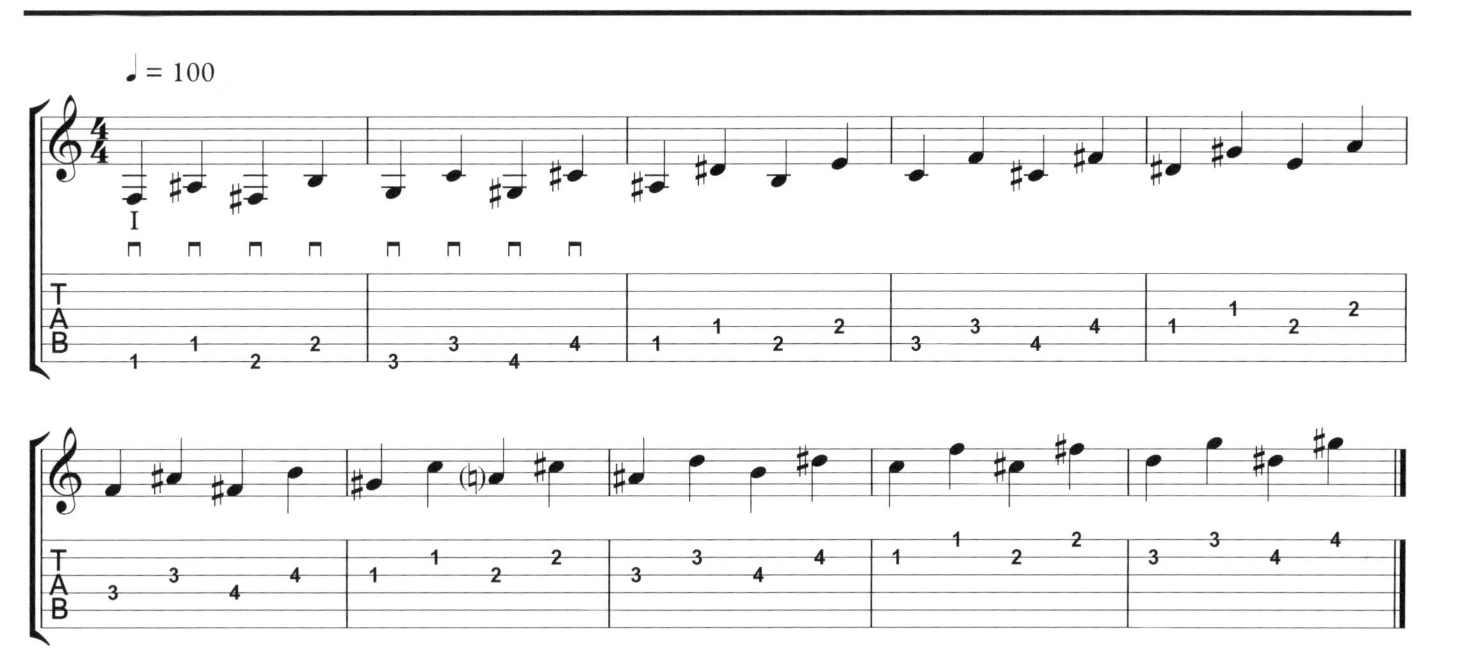

DATE OF COMPLETION: ______________________

LEVEL 1: EXERCISE 9

This exercise will train each finger to roll in reverse, to the same fret of the next lowest string. Play each initial note with your finger flattened, then roll to your fingertip on the next lowest string. Try to play legato, connecting all notes together with no gaps of sound. Roll each of your fingers from string to string, paying careful attention that you are connecting all notes together with no gaps of sound.

DATE OF COMPLETION: ____________________

LEVEL 1: EXERCISE 10

Roll each of your fingers from string to string, paying careful attention that you are connecting all notes together with no gaps of sound. Upon reaching the B-string and high E-string, move up to second position and play the pattern in reverse from the high E-string. This pattern may be played up the entire length of the neck.

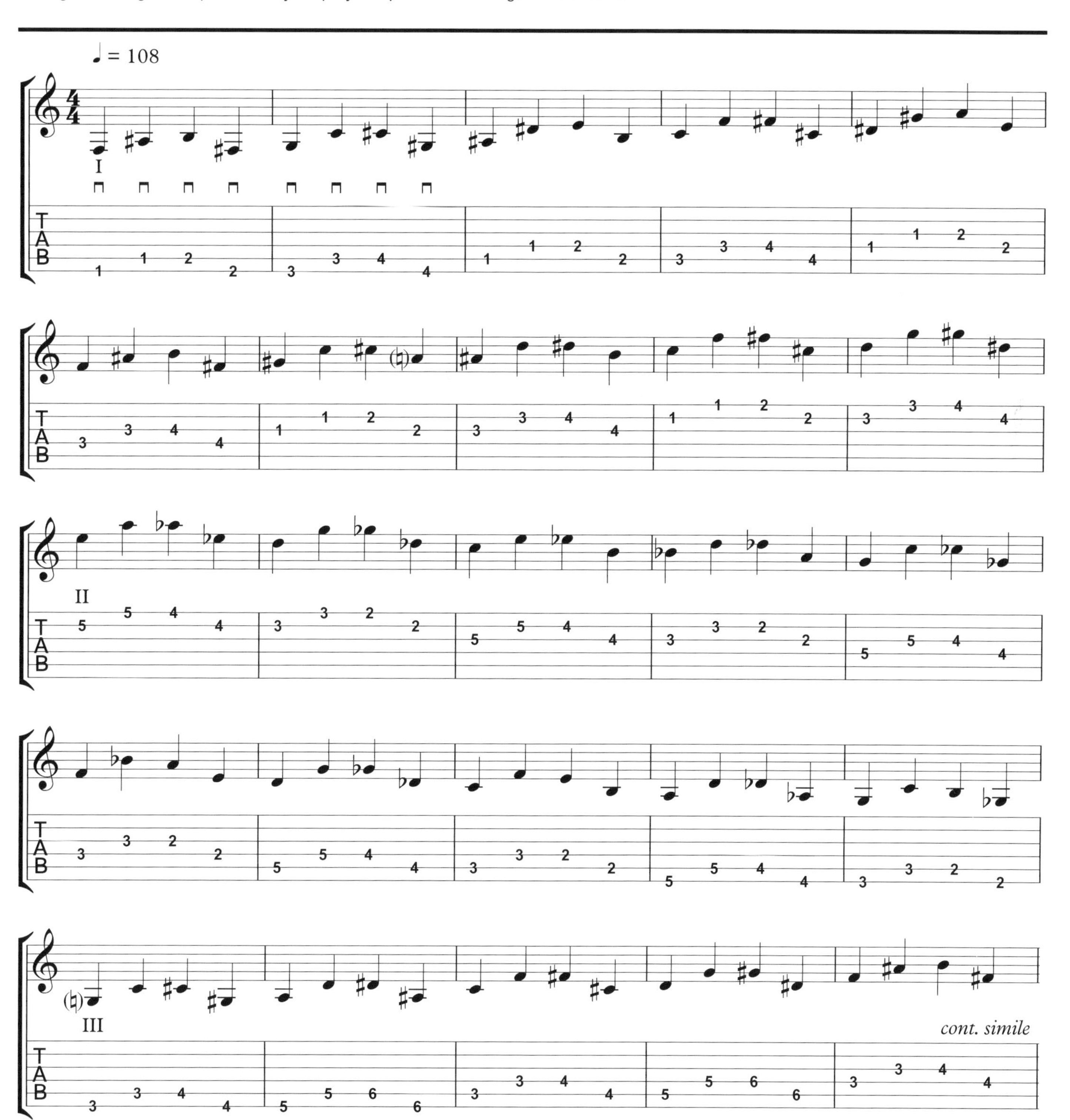

DATE OF COMPLETION: ____________________

LEVEL 1: EXERCISE 11

This exercise will introduce the technique of legato slides, which are notated as a diagonal line between the notes (or numbers in TAB) accompanied by a curved line enclosing the notes (or numbers). To play a legato slide, pick the first note and then slide the same finger across the string into the fret of the next note (which may be higher or lower). The next note should not be picked, but should continue to resonate as long as you have continuous pressure on the string. Because your hand will be moving back and forth to play these slides, hand positions will be notated throughout so you will always have a reference of where your hand should be on the neck. Remember, hand positions are a reference of where your first finger should be located on the neck.

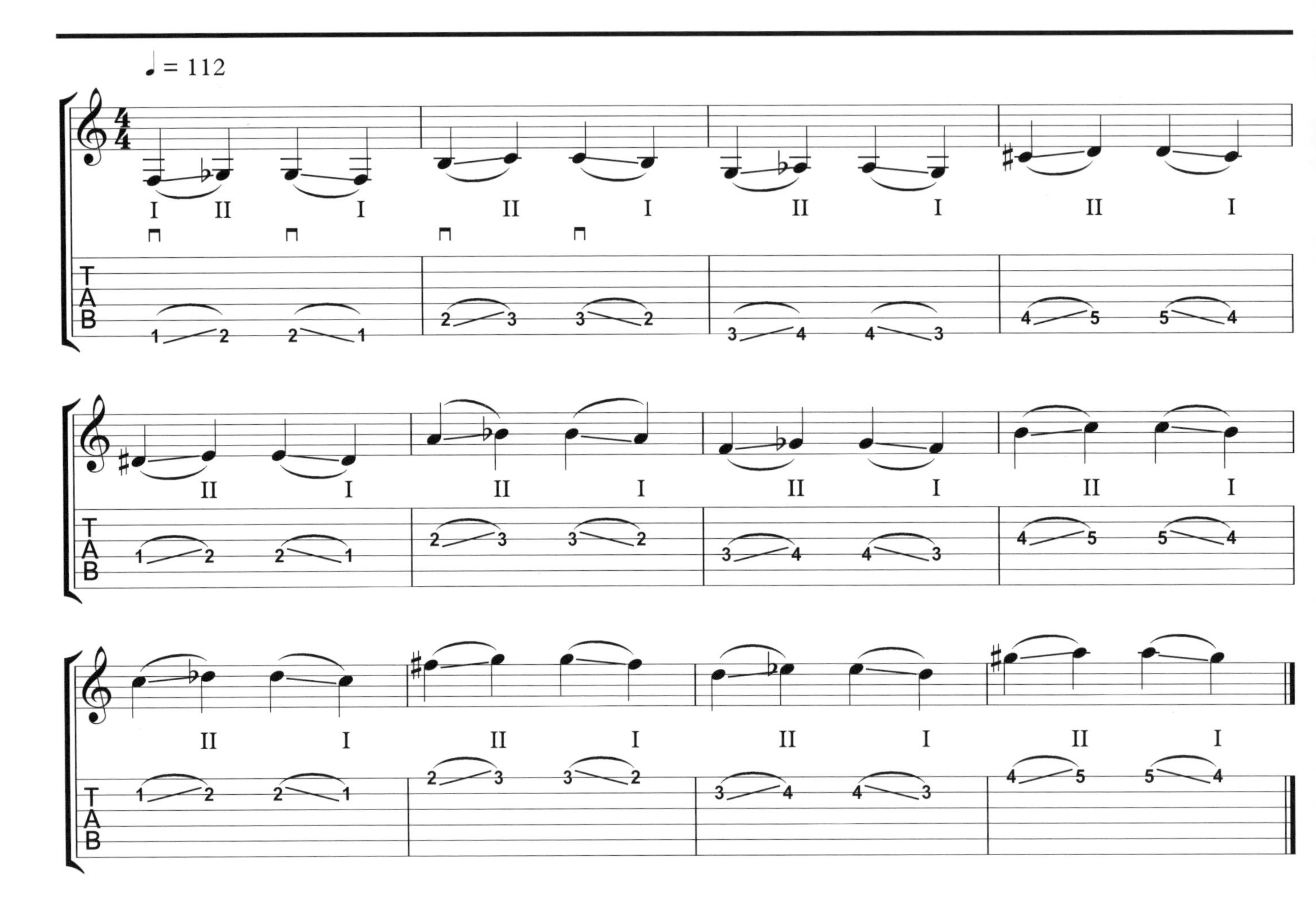

DATE OF COMPLETION: ____________________

LEVEL 1: EXERCISE 12

This exercise will introduce the technique of hammer-ons, which are notated as curved lines enclosing the notes (or numbers in TAB). To play a hammer-on, pick the first note and then "hammer" the appropriate finger onto the next note. The next note should not be picked, but should continue to resonate as long as you quickly hammer-on your finger with adequate pressure. Hammer-ons can only go from lower notes to higher notes on the same string.

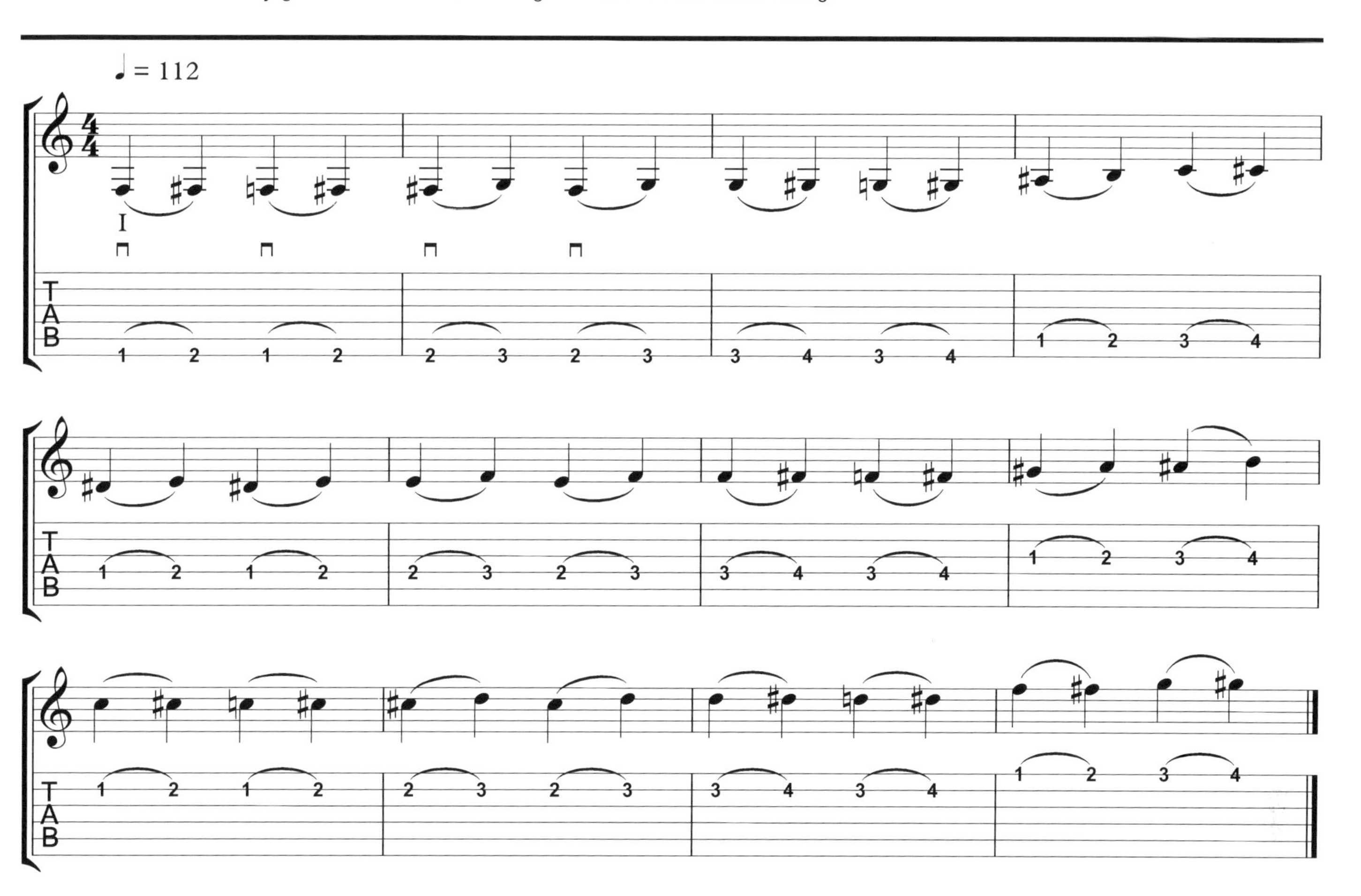

LEVEL 1: EXERCISE 13

This exercise will introduce the technique of pull-offs, which are notated as curved lines enclosing the notes (or numbers in TAB). To play a pull-off, pick the first note and then "pull" your finger off of the string to access the next note, which should already be in place. The second note should not be picked, but should continue to resonate as long as the string is adequately pulled. Realize that simply releasing your finger from the string is not a pull-off – you must actually pull the string a bit! Although the notation of pull-offs is the same as hammer-ons, they should not be confused because hammer-ons can only move to higher notes and pull-offs can only move to lower notes.

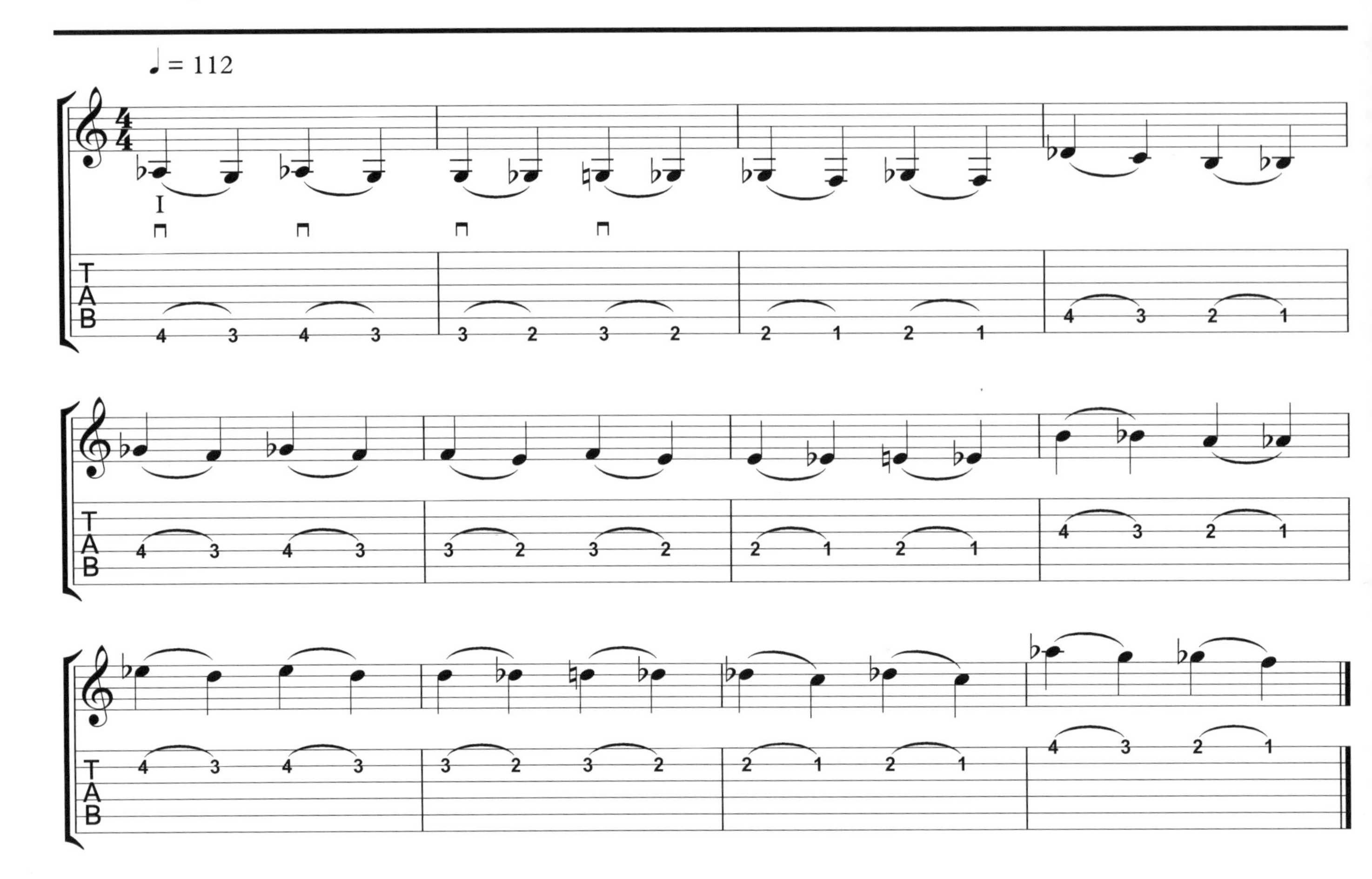

 DATE OF COMPLETION: ____________________

LEVEL 1: EXERCISE 14

This exercise will focus on string skipping, in which you will have to skip over a string while continuously playing. Upon completing the finger pattern in first position, move up to second position and play the pattern in reverse from the high E-string. This pattern may be played up the entire length of the neck.

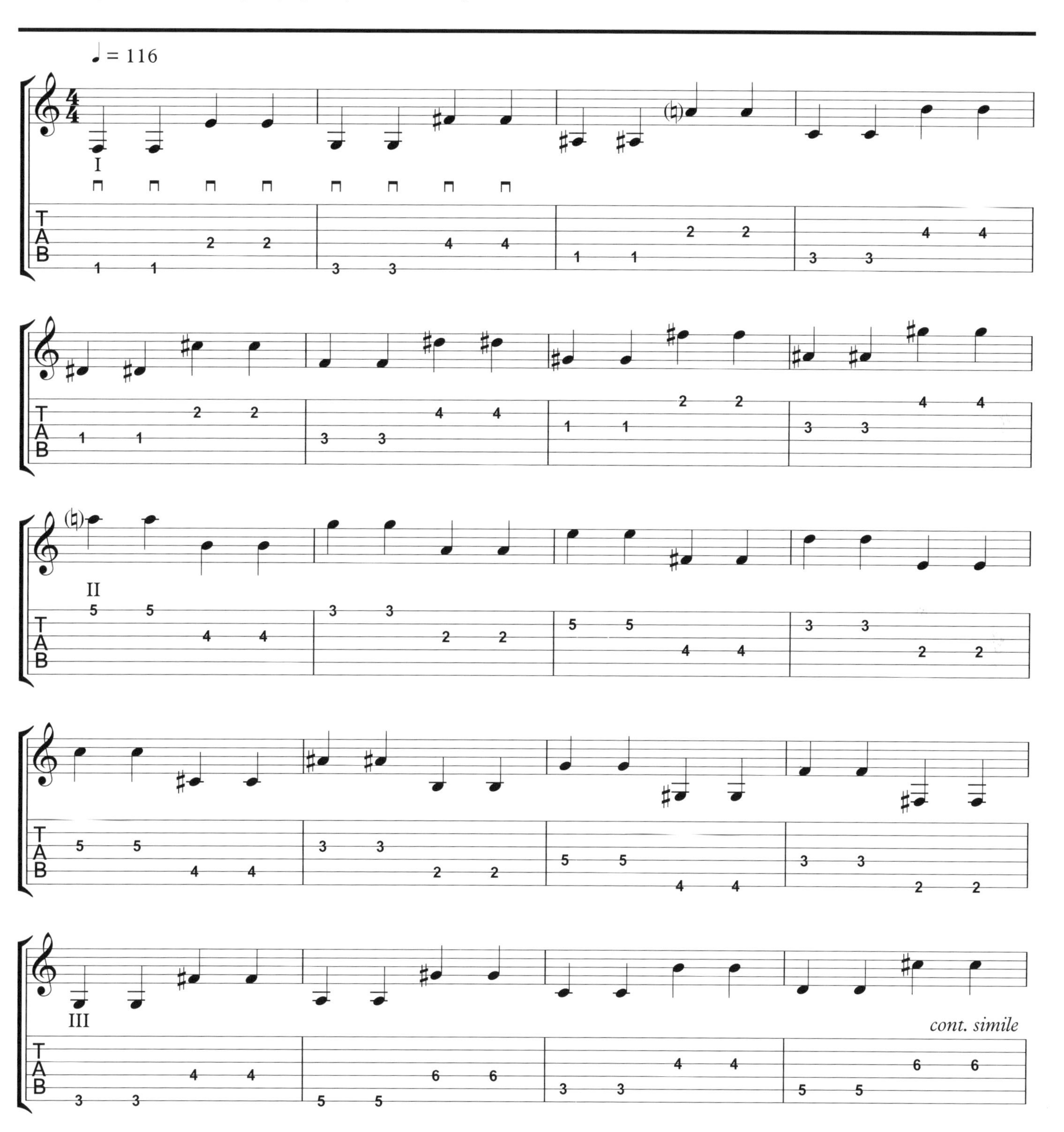

DATE OF COMPLETION: ______________________________

LEVEL 1: EXERCISE 15

This exercise will combine string skipping and finger rolls to help solidify both techniques. Pay careful attention to roll finger 1 or finger 4 when switching to an adjacent string. This will involve sometimes starting the roll with a fingertip and sometimes starting the roll with a flattened finger. Upon completing the finger pattern in first position, move up to second position and play the pattern starting from the high E-string. This pattern may be played up the entire length of the neck.

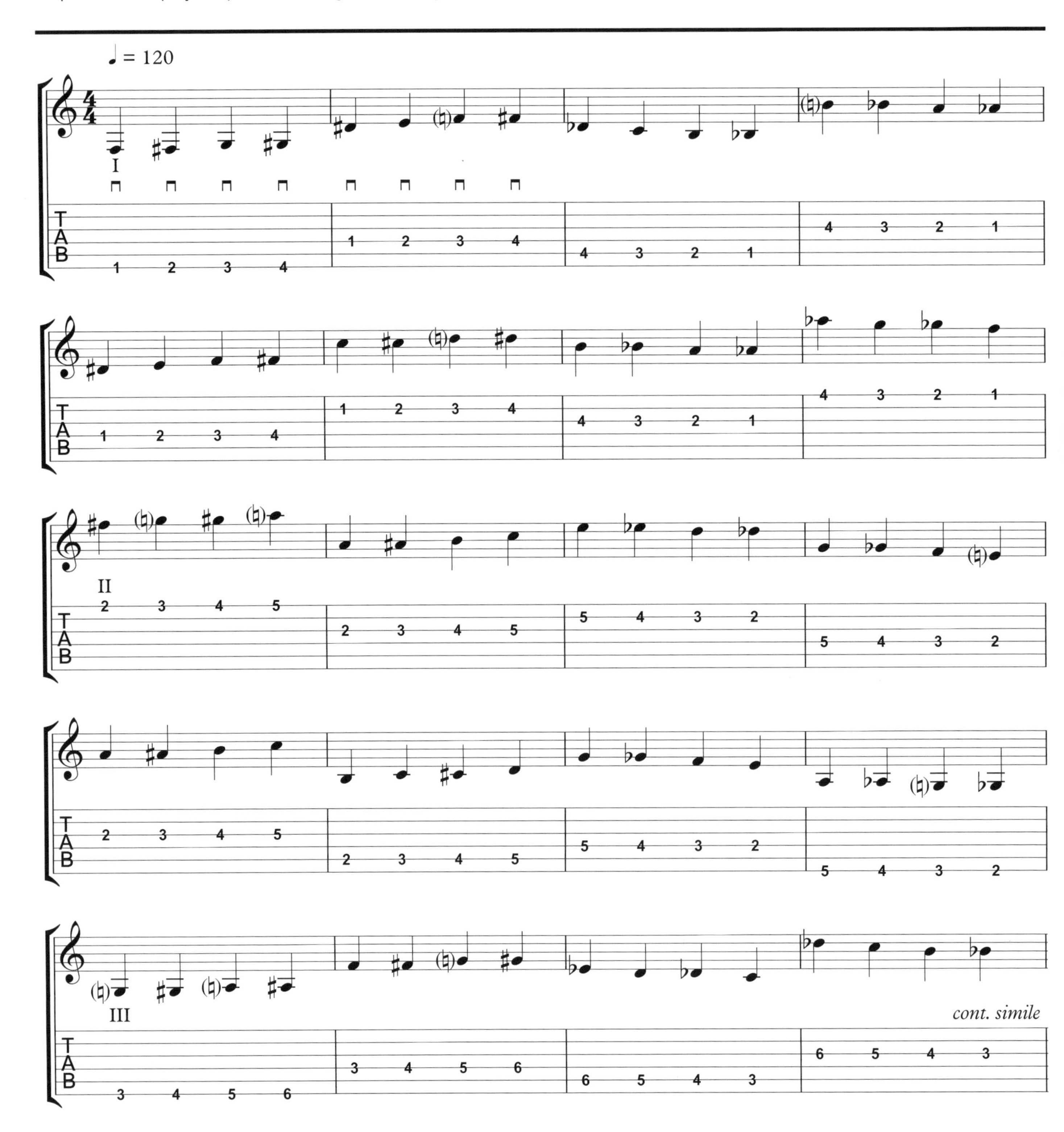

DATE OF COMPLETION: ____________________

LEVEL 1: EXERCISE 16

This exercise combines string switching with slides up and down for all fingers, along with a few finger rolls for the first finger. Because your hand will be moving back and forth to play these slides, hand positions will be notated throughout so you will always have a reference of where your hand should be on the neck. This pattern may be played in repetition by playing from the last measure to the first measure without a break.

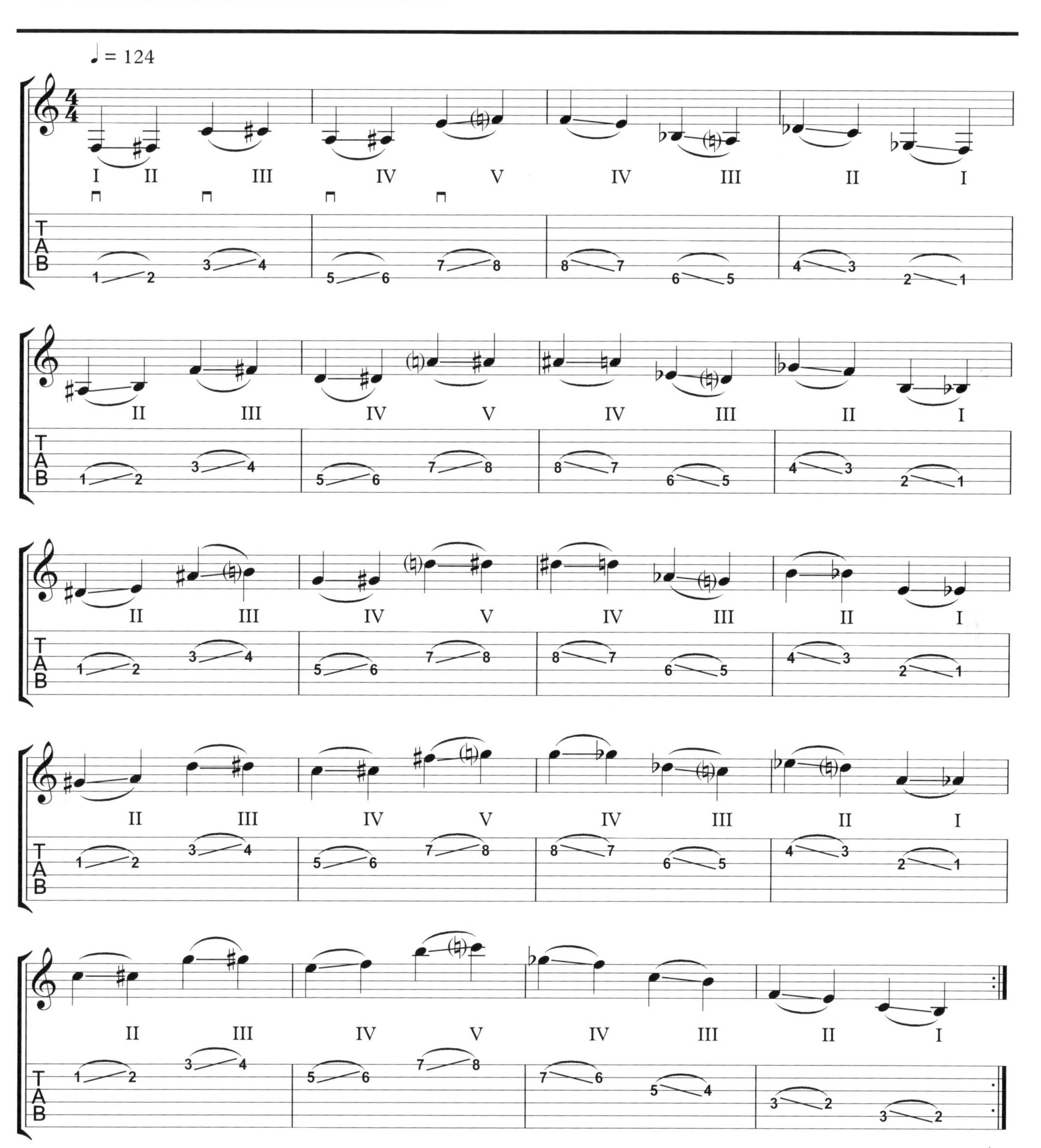

LEVEL 1: EXERCISE 17

This exercise will include every possible finger combination for hammer-ons. Be sure that every hammer-on note is clearly audible by quickly hammering your finger onto the string with adequate pressure. This exercise may be be played in repetition and may begin at any hand position on the neck.

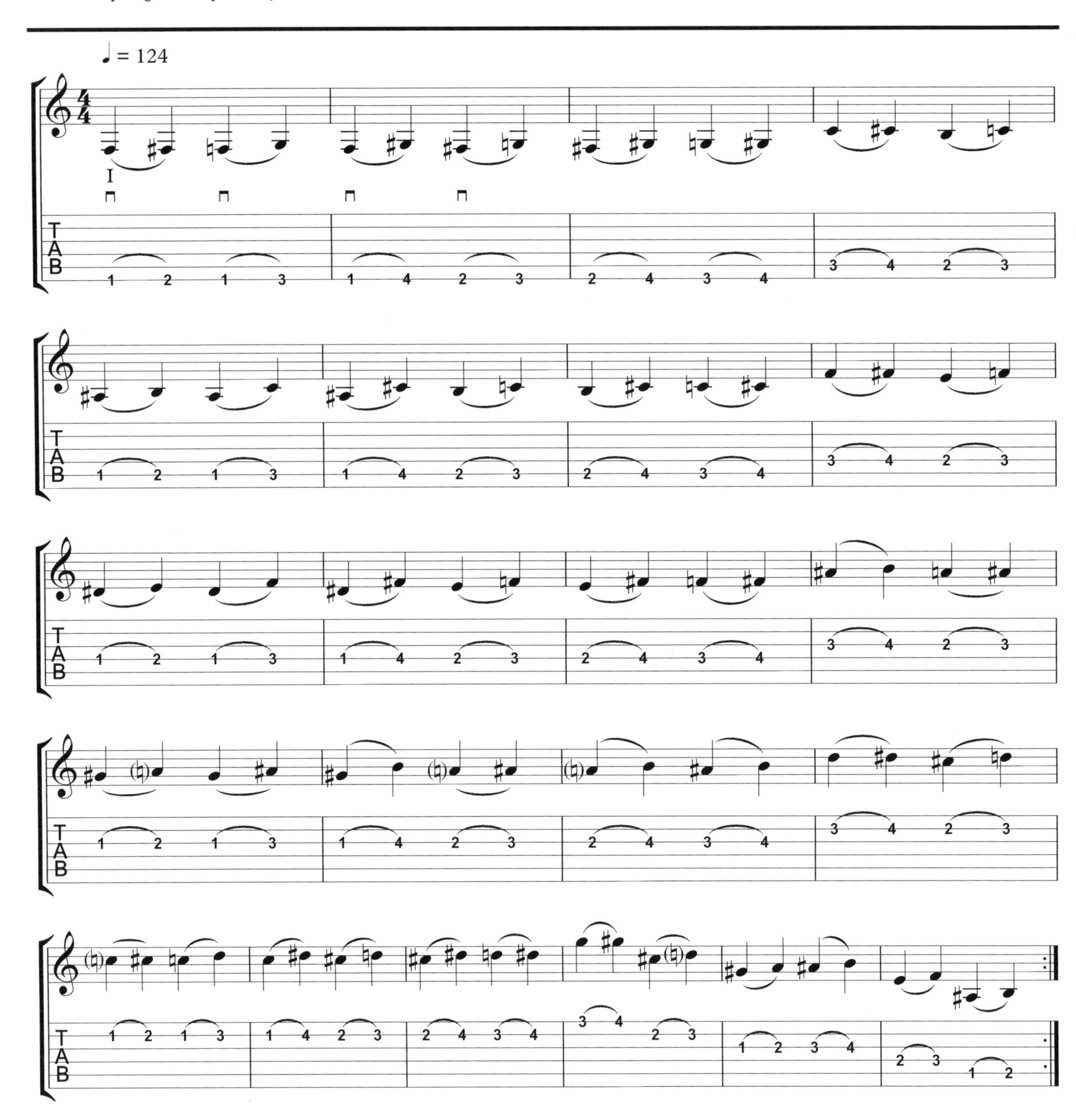

DATE OF COMPLETION: ___________________

LEVEL 1: EXERCISE 18

This exercise will include every possible finger combination for pull-offs. Be sure that every pull-off note is clearly audible by slightly pulling your finger off of the string, with the next note already in place. This exercise may be played in repetition and may begin at any hand position on the neck.

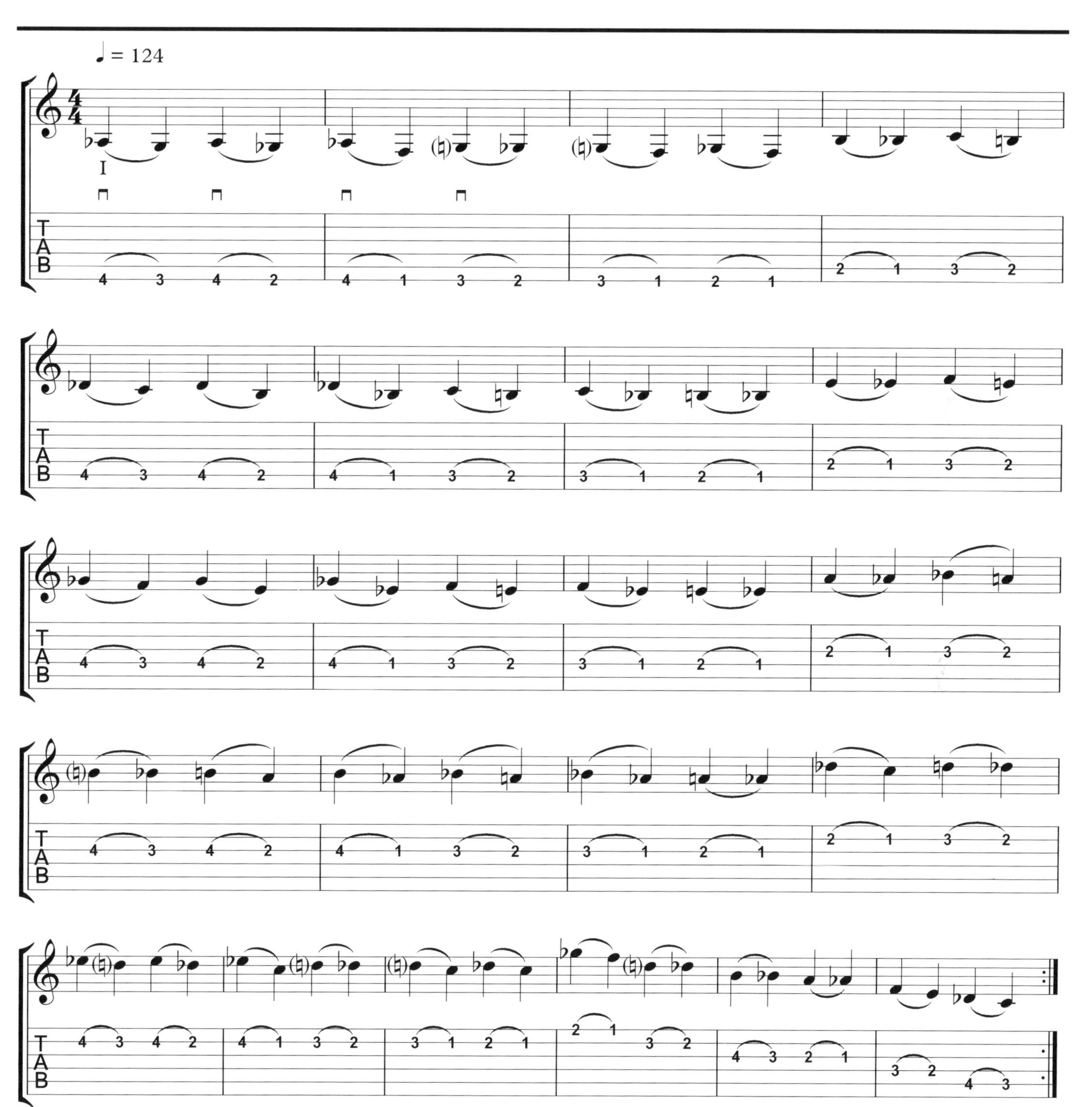

LEVEL 1: EXERCISE 19

This exercise will focus on string skipping, with the finger pattern 1-3-2-4. Upon completing the finger pattern in first position, move up to second position and play the pattern in reverse from the high E-string. This pattern may be played up the entire length of the neck.

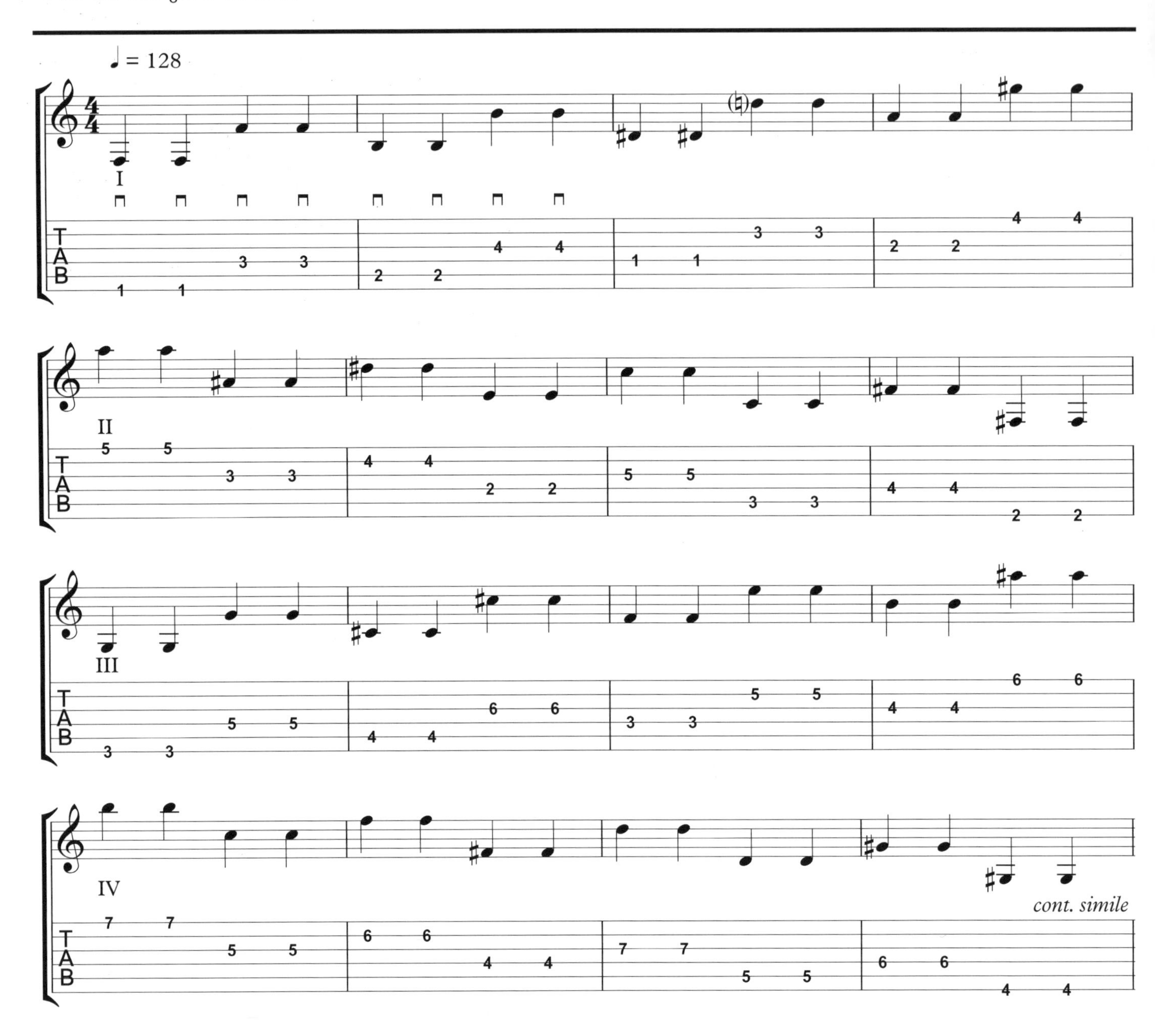

DATE OF COMPLETION: ____________________

LEVEL 1: EXERCISE 20

This exercise includes a combination of string skipping and finger rolls. Pay careful attention to roll finger 1 or finger 4 when switching to an adjacent string. Upon completing the finger pattern in first position, move up to second position and play the pattern starting from the high E-string. This pattern may be played up the entire length of the neck.

DATE OF COMPLETION: ______________________________

MUSIC NOTATION: EIGHTH NOTES

Eighth notes are half the value of quarter notes, which means that an eighth note will receive half of a beat in a 2/4, 3/4 or 4/4 time signature. These notes will allow for more speed, as the notes are twice as fast as quarter notes. In standard music notation, eighth notes will often times be grouped together by use of a beam.

Eighth notes are represented as

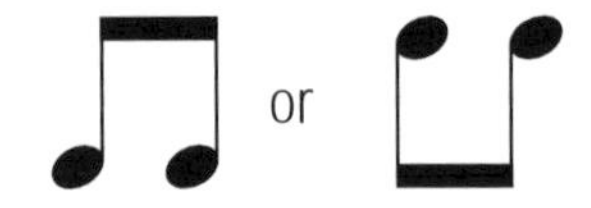

COUNTING EIGHTH NOTES

When counting a rhythm which contains two consecutive eighth notes, one of the eighth notes will occur on a beat, and the other will occur between the beats. The eighth note that occurs on the beat should be counted with the appropriate beat number (1, 2, 3 or 4), while the other eighth note should be counted as "and" (notated "&"). Below are two examples of the appropriate method that should be used for counting eighth notes.

LEVEL 1: EXERCISE 21

To prepare yourself for eighth note finger exercises, you should first accurately train your picking hand. Eighth notes require the use of alternate picking, which includes both downstrokes (⊓) and upstrokes (V). For this exercise, pick four times on each string of the guitar, ensuring that you are playing the eighth notes evenly by using downstrokes when playing on the beats and upstrokes halfway in between each beat. This exercise may be played in repetition by playing from the last measure to the first measure without a break.

LEVEL 1: EXERCISE 22

For this picking exercise, pick only two times on each string before switching to the adjacent higher or lower string. Continue to play the eighth notes evenly by using downstrokes when playing on the beats and upstrokes halfway in between each beat. This exercise may be played in repetition by playing from the last measure to the first measure without a break.

DATE OF COMPLETION: ______________________

LEVEL 1: EXERCISE 23

Starting on the low E-string and using downstrokes and upstrokes, alternate the finger patterns 4-3-2-1 and 1-2-3-4 while switching strings using finger rolls. Upon completing the pattern in first position, move up to second position and play the finger pattern again starting from the high E-string, and continuing to use finger rolls when switching strings. This exercise may be played up the entire length of the guitar neck.

DATE OF COMPLETION: ______________________

LEVEL 1: EXERCISE 24

Starting on the low E-string and using downstrokes and upstrokes, alternate the finger patterns 4-2-3-1 and 1-3-2-4 while switching strings using finger rolls. Upon completing the pattern in first position, move up to second position and play the finger pattern again starting from the high E-string, and continuing to use finger rolls when switching strings. This exercise may be played up the entire length of the guitar neck.

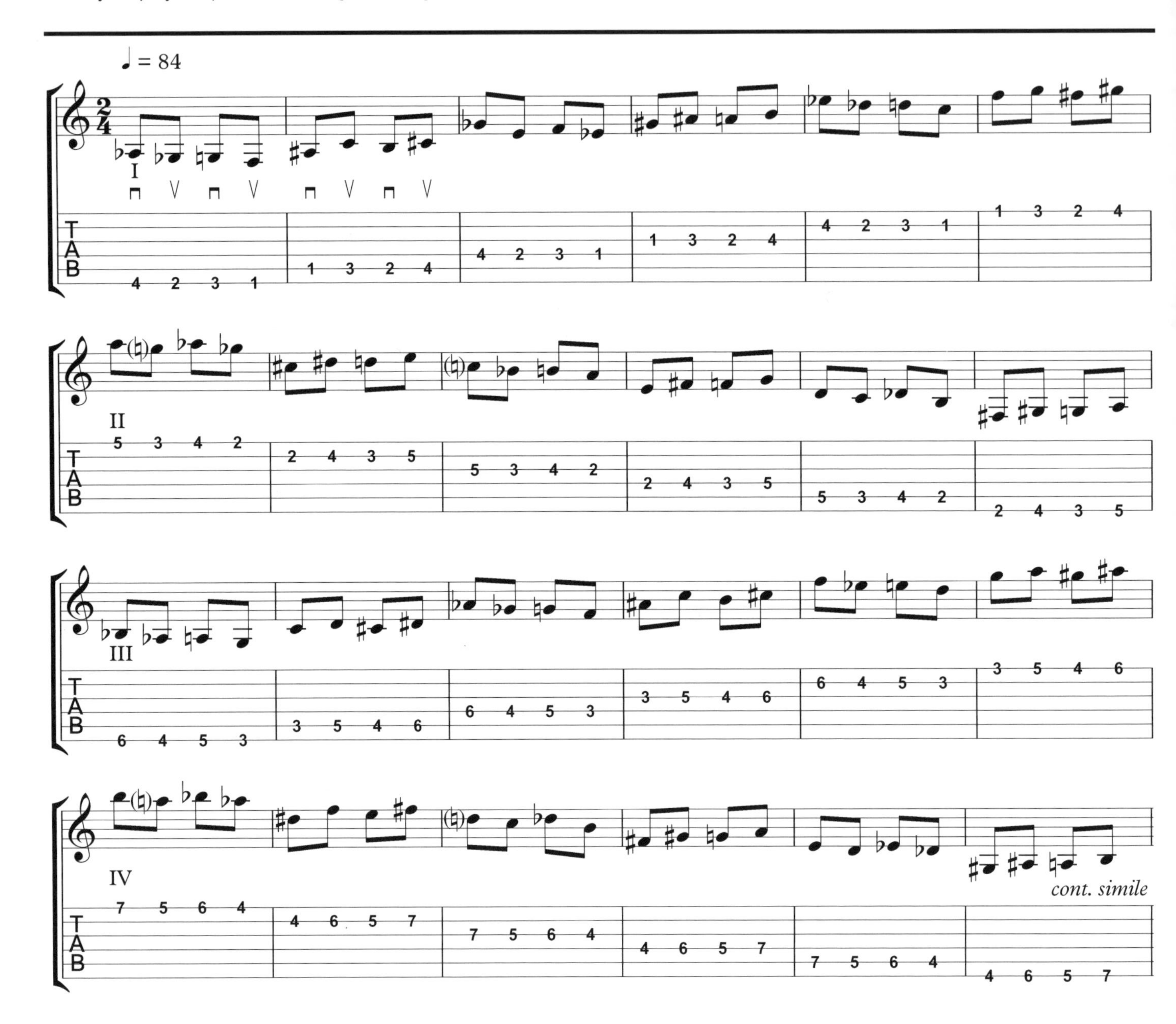

DATE OF COMPLETION: ______________________

LEVEL 2: EXERCISE 25

Starting on the low E-string and using alternate picking, alternate the finger patterns 1-2-3-4 and 4-3-2-1 while switching strings mid-measure. Be sure to use finger rolls when switching to an adjacent string with the same finger. Upon completing the pattern in first position, move up to second position and play the finger pattern again starting from the high E-string. This exercise may be played up the entire length of the guitar neck.

DATE OF COMPLETION: ______________________

LEVEL 2: EXERCISE 26

Starting on the low E-string and using alternate picking, alternate the finger patterns 1-3-2-4 and 4-2-3-1 while switching strings mid-measure. Be sure to use finger rolls when switching to an adjacent string with the same finger. Upon completing the pattern in first position, move up to second position and play the finger pattern again from the high E-string. This exercise may be played up the entire length of the guitar neck.

DATE OF COMPLETION: ______________________

LEVEL 2: EXERCISE 27

This exercise will include a combination of legato slides and string switching. Each slide begins on a beat, so only downstrokes are needed. Because these are legato slides, you do not need to pick the second note of the slide. Before completing the slide sequence on the B-string and high E-string, omit the last slide to stay in second position and play the pattern again from the high E-string. This exercise may be played up the entire length of the guitar neck.

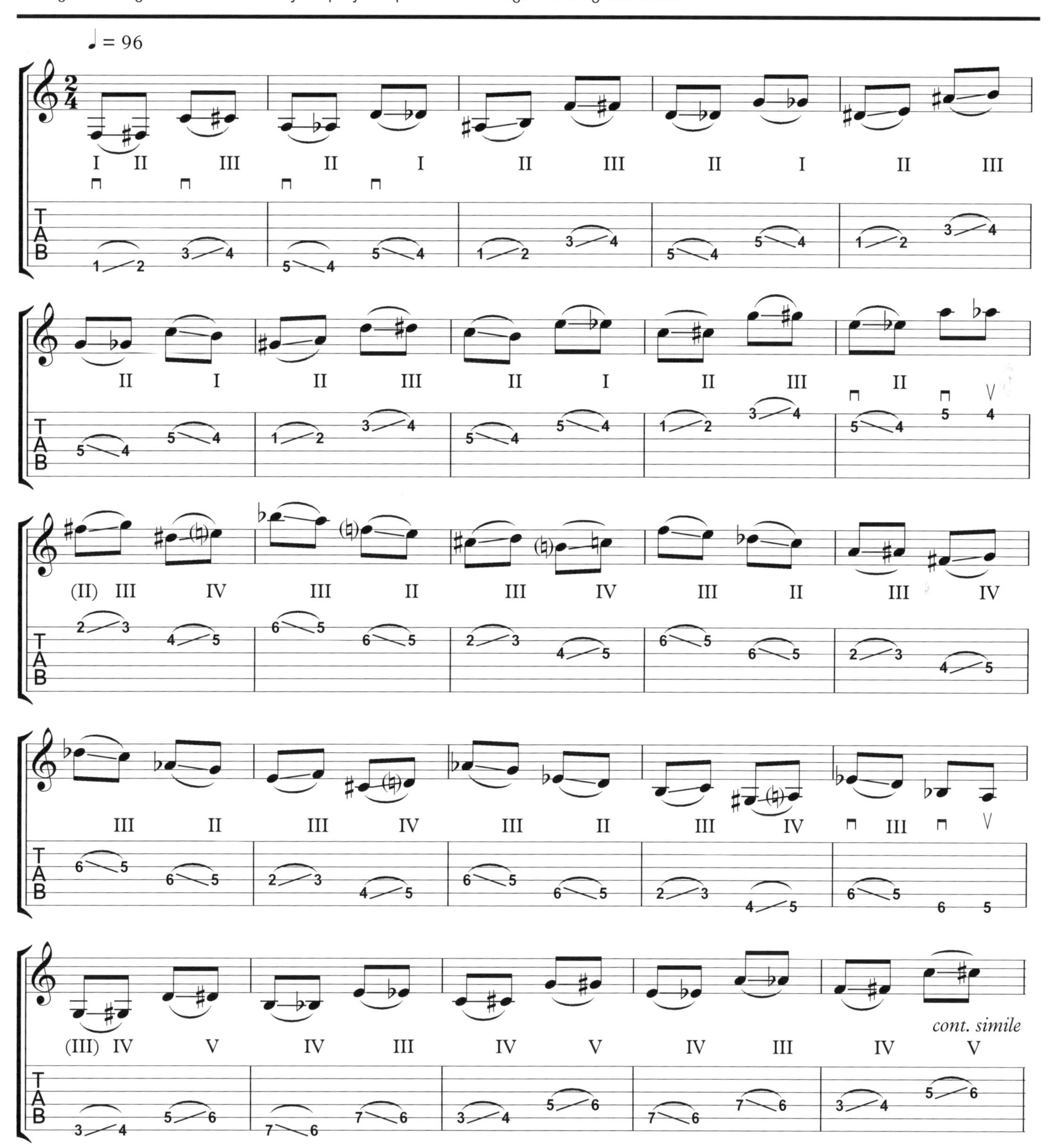

DATE OF COMPLETION: ______________________

LEVEL 2: EXERCISE 28

This exercise will include a combination of hammer-ons and string switching, using the finger pattern 1-2-3-4. Because each hammer-on begins on a beat, only downstrokes are needed. You do not need to pick the second note of a hammer-on, but should instead use your finger as a "hammer." Before completing the hammer-on sequence on the B-string and high E-string, replace the last hammer-on with an upward slide into second position and play the pattern again from the high E-string. This exercise may be played up the entire length of the guitar neck.

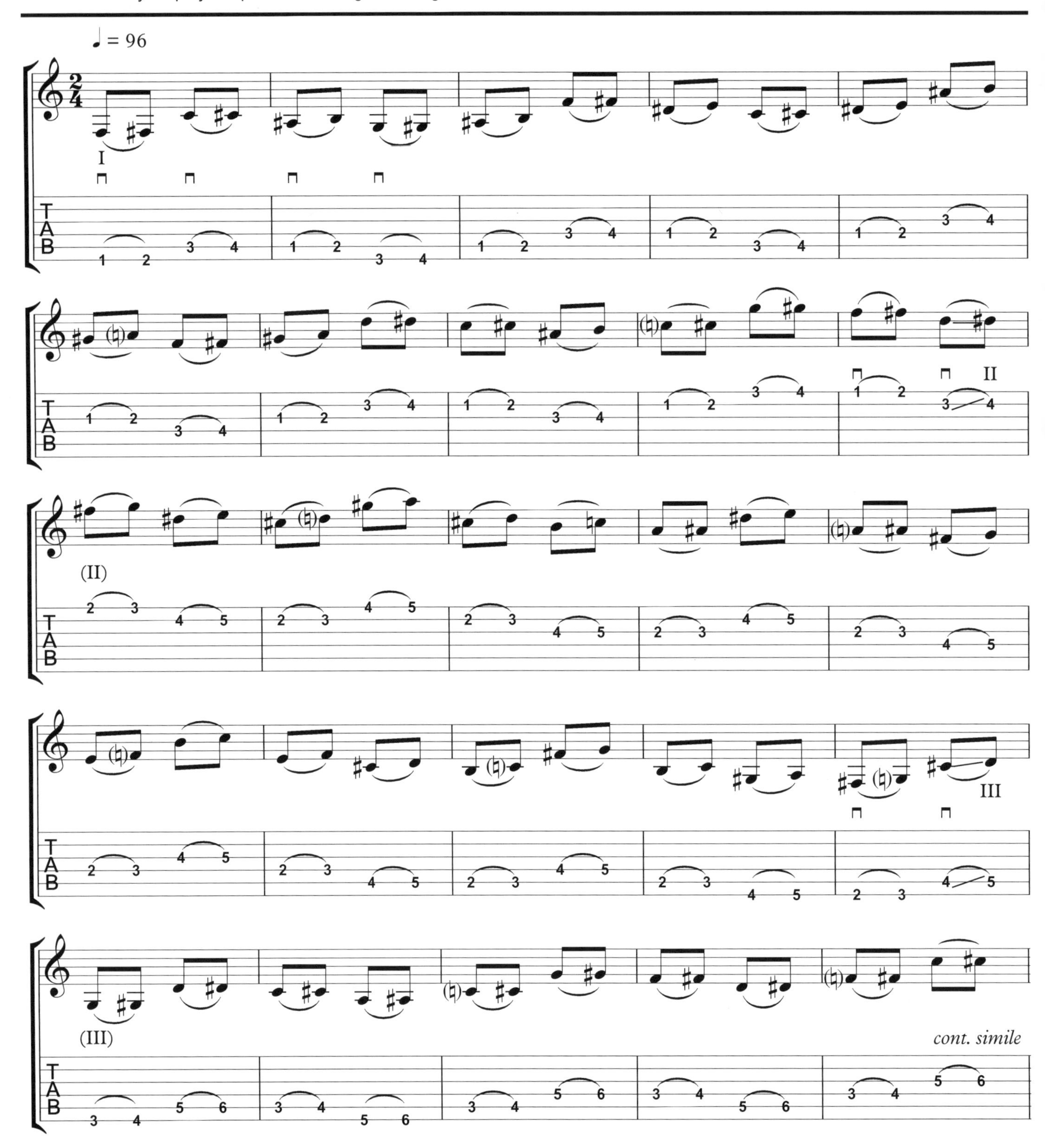

DATE OF COMPLETION: ___________________

LEVEL 2: EXERCISE 29

This exercise will include a combination of pull-offs and string switching, using the finger pattern 4-3-2-1. Because each pull-off begins on a beat, only downstrokes are needed. You do not need to pick the second note of a pull-off, but should instead "pull" your finger off of the string. Before completing the pull-off sequence on the B-string and high E-string, replace the last pull-off with an upward slide into second position and play the pattern again from the high E-string. This exercise may be played up the entire length of the guitar neck.

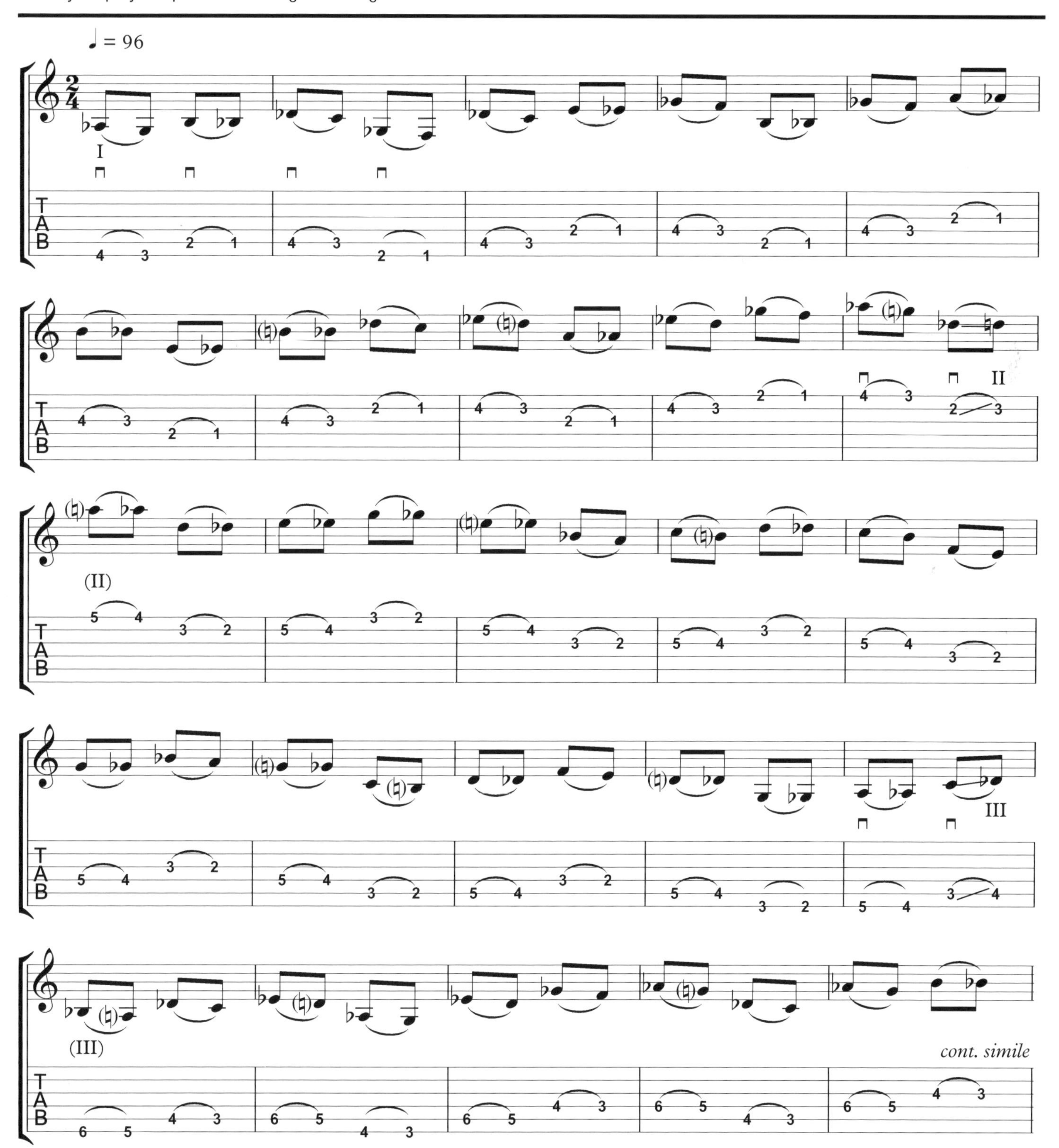

DATE OF COMPLETION: ______________________

LEVEL 2: EXERCISE 30

This exercises contains alternating hammer-ons and pull-offs combined with string switching, using the finger pattern 1-2-4-3. Because each hammer-on and pull-off will begin on a beat, only downstrokes are needed. Before completing the hammer-on and pull-off sequence on the B-string and E-string, replace the last pull-off with an upward slide into second position and play the reverse finger pattern from the high E-string. This exercise may be played up the entire length of the guitar neck.

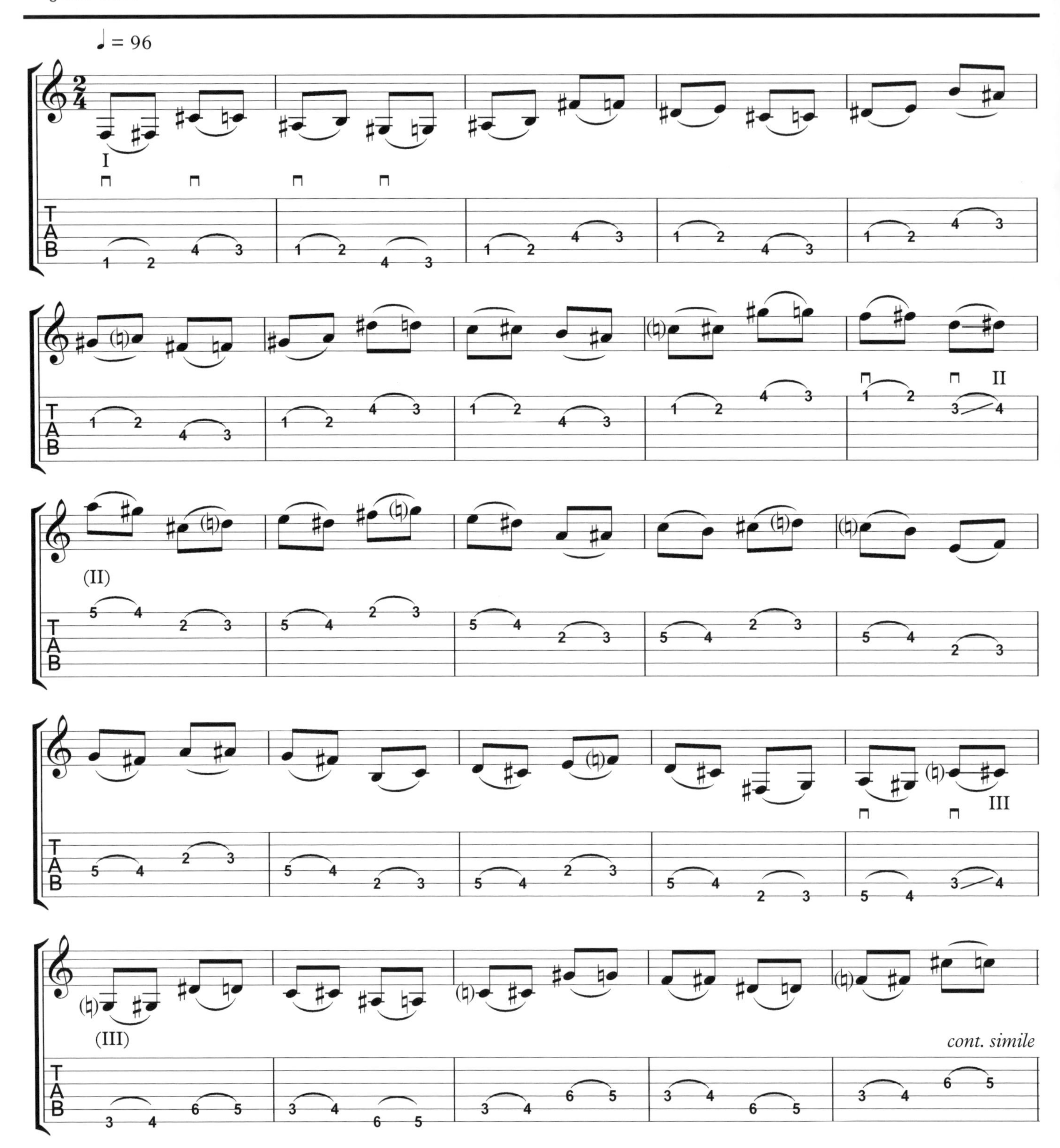

DATE OF COMPLETION: ______________________

LEVEL 2: EXERCISE 31

This exercise will include a combination of legato slides and string switching, in which you will constantly alternate upward slides and downward slides. Because each slide begins on a beat, only downstrokes are needed. Before completing the slide sequence on the B-string and high E-string, omit the last slide to stay in second position and play the pattern again from the high E-string. This exercise may be played up the entire length of the guitar neck.

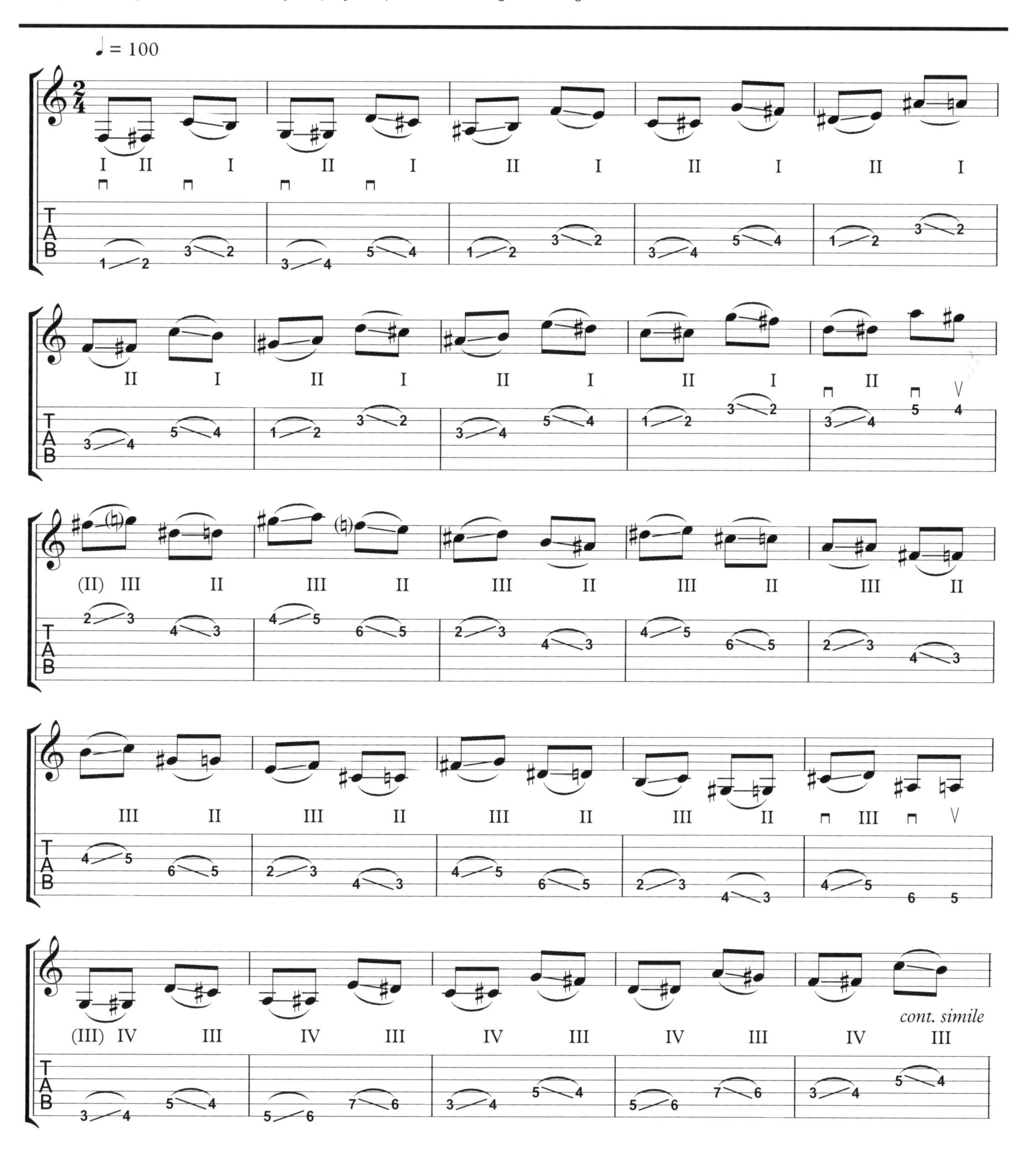

LEVEL 2: EXERCISE 32

This exercise will include a combination of hammer-ons and string switching, using the finger pattern 1-3-2-4. Because each hammer-on begins on a beat, only downstrokes are needed. Before completing the hammer-on sequence on the B-string and high E-string, replace the last hammer-on with an upward slide into second position and play the pattern again from the high E-string. This exercise may be played up the entire length of the guitar neck.

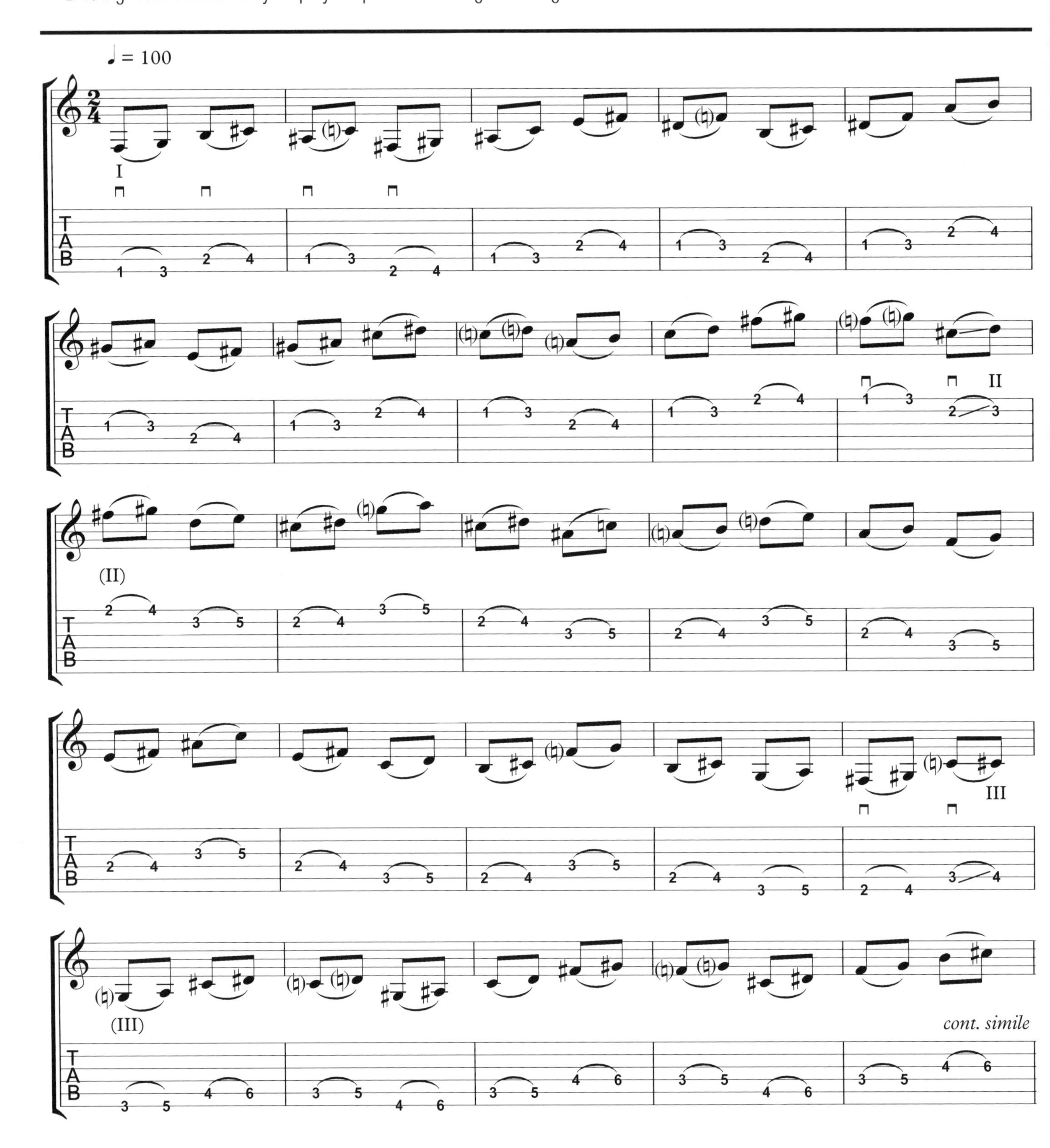

DATE OF COMPLETION: ______________________

LEVEL 2: EXERCISE 33

This exercise will include a combination of pull-offs and string switching, using the finger pattern 4-2-3-1. Because each pull-off begins on a beat, only downstrokes are needed. Before completing the pull-off sequence on the B-string and high E-string, replace the last pull-off with an upward slide into second position and play the pattern again from the high E-string. This exercise may be played up the entire length of the guitar neck.

DATE OF COMPLETION: ____________________

LEVEL 2: EXERCISE 34

This exercises contains alternating hammer-ons and pull-offs combined with string switching, using the finger pattern 1-3-4-2. Because each hammer-on and pull-off will begin on a beat, only downstrokes are needed. Before completing the hammer-on and pull-off sequence on the B-string and E-string, replace the last pull-off with an upward slide into second position and play the reverse finger pattern starting from the high E-string. This exercise may be played up the entire length of the guitar neck.

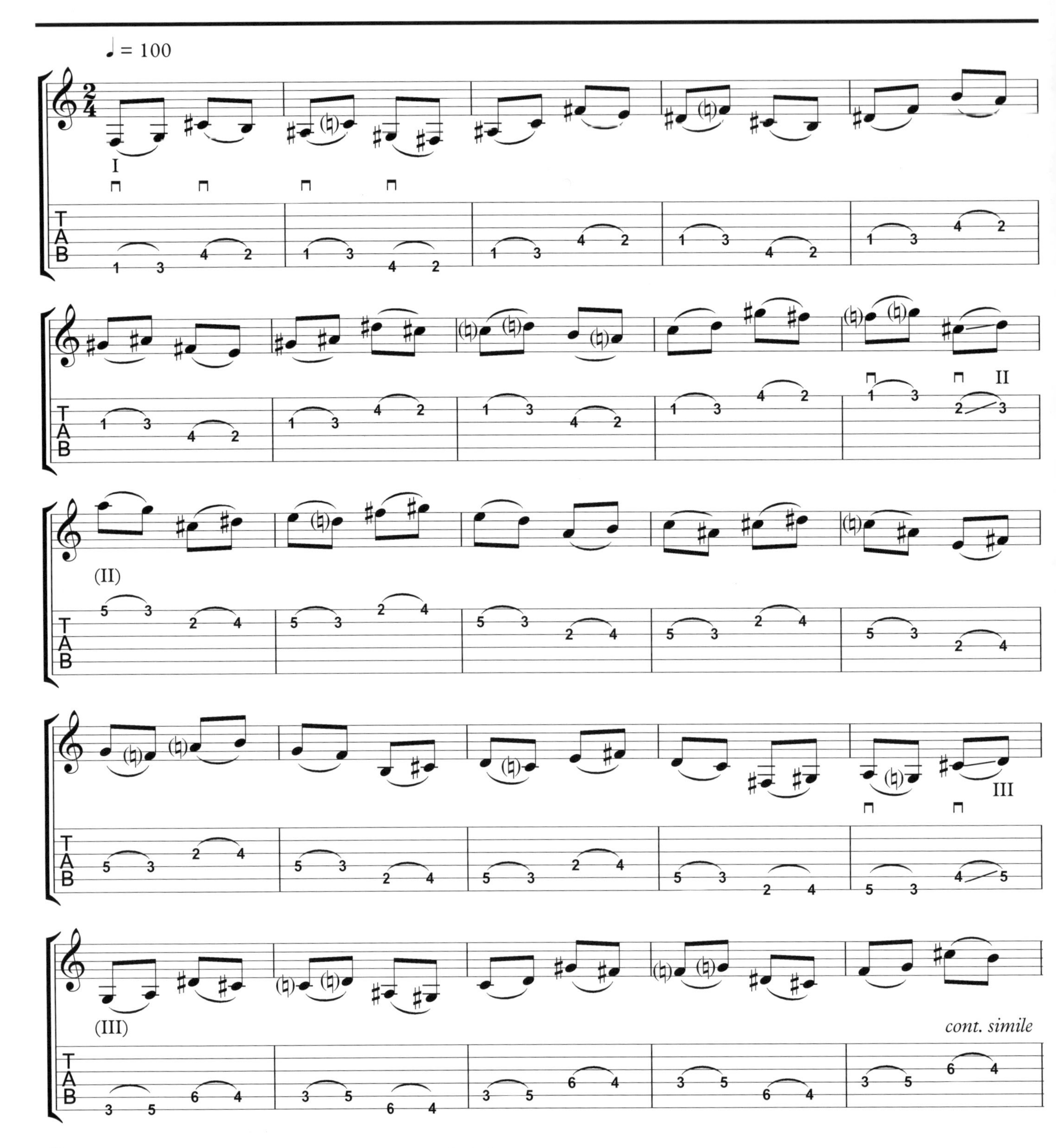

DATE OF COMPLETION: ______________________

LEVEL 2: EXERCISE 35

This exercise will focus on string skipping and alternate picking, with the finger pattern 1-2-4-3. Before completing the finger pattern in first position, replace the last picked note with an upward slide into second position and play the reverse finger pattern starting from the high E-string. This exercise may be played up the entire length of the guitar neck.

DATE OF COMPLETION: ____________________

LEVEL 2: EXERCISE 36

When playing eighth notes, it is sometimes necessary to switch strings in between the beats, on an upstroke. To train your picking hand to continuously use alternate picking in these instances, pick each string three times before switching to the adjacent higher or lower string. Pay careful attention that you are using alternate picking the entire time by using downstrokes on the beats and upstrokes halfway in between each beat. This exercise may be played in repetition by playing from the last measure to the first measure without a break.

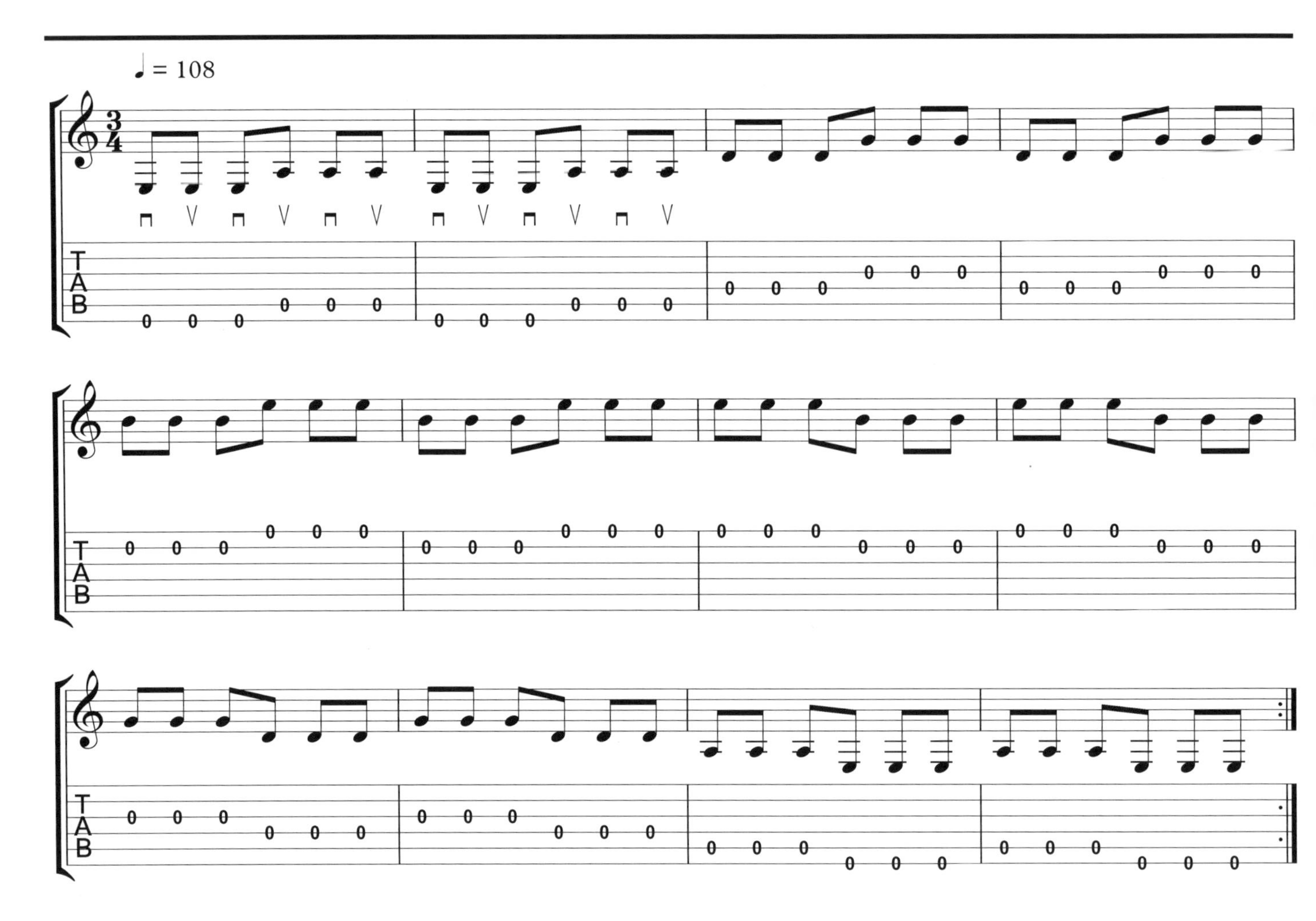

DATE OF COMPLETION: ____________________

LEVEL 2: EXERCISE 37

For this exercise, pick each string only once before switching to the adjacent higher or lower string. Pay careful attention that you are using alternate picking the entire time by using downstrokes on the beats and upstrokes halfway in between each beat. This exercise may be played in repetition by playing from the last measure to the first measure without a break.

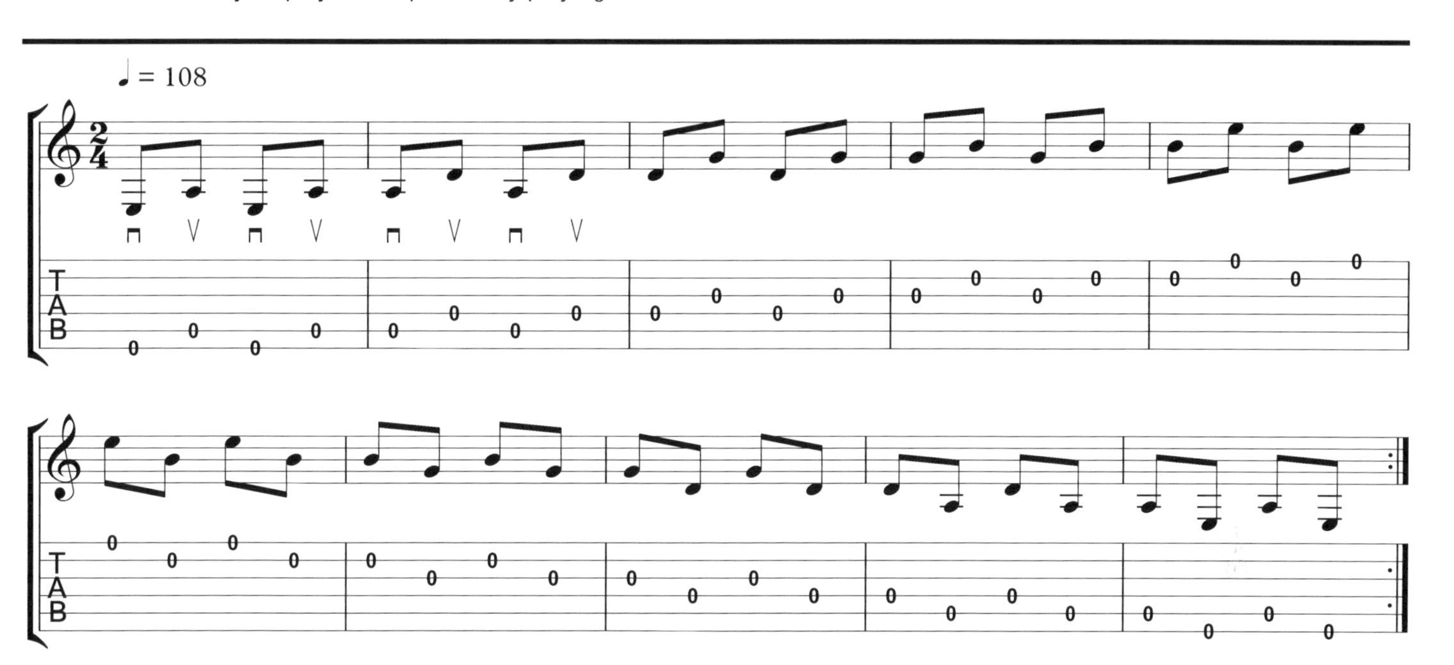

DATE OF COMPLETION: ______________________

LEVEL 2: EXERCISE 38

Starting on the low E-string and using alternate picking, play three notes per string while alternating the finger patterns 1-2-3 and 2-3-4. Upon completing the pattern in first position, move up to second position and play the reverse finger patterns from the high E-string. This exercise may be played up the entire length of the guitar neck.

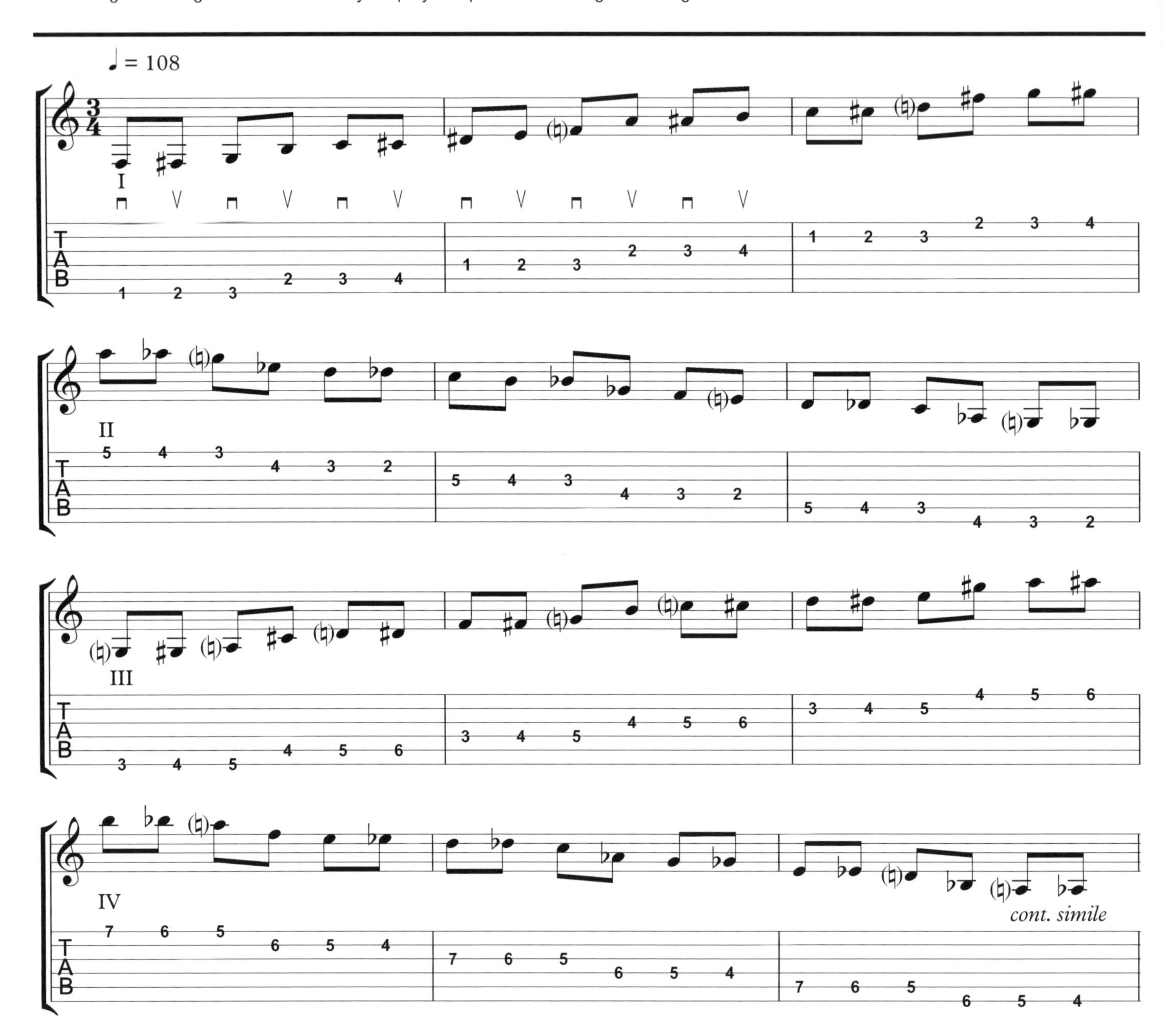

DATE OF COMPLETION: ____________________

LEVEL 2: EXERCISE 39

Starting on the low E-string and using alternate picking, play three notes per string while alternating the finger patterns 1-2-3 and 4-3-2. Before completing the pattern in first position, alter the last finger pattern to 4-3-1 in order to move up to second position and play the finger patterns again from the high E-string. This exercise may be played up the entire length of the guitar neck.

DATE OF COMPLETION: ____________________

LEVEL 2: EXERCISE 40

This exercise will combine alternate picking with very frequent string switching, using the finger pattern 1-2-3-4. Upon completing the finger pattern on the B-string and E-string, move up to second position and play the reverse finger pattern from the high E-string. Pay careful attention that you are using alternate picking the entire time by using downstrokes on the beats and upstrokes halfway in between each beat. This exercise may be played up the entire length of the guitar neck.

DATE OF COMPLETION: ____________________

LEVEL 2: EXERCISE 41

This exercise combines alternate picking, string switching and finger rolls, using the finger pattern 1-2-3-4. Upon completing the finger pattern on the B-string and high E-string, move up to second position and play the reverse finger pattern from the B-string. Pay careful attention that you are using alternate picking the entire time, and that your fingers always roll to the adjacent higher or lower string. This exercise may be played up the entire length of the guitar neck.

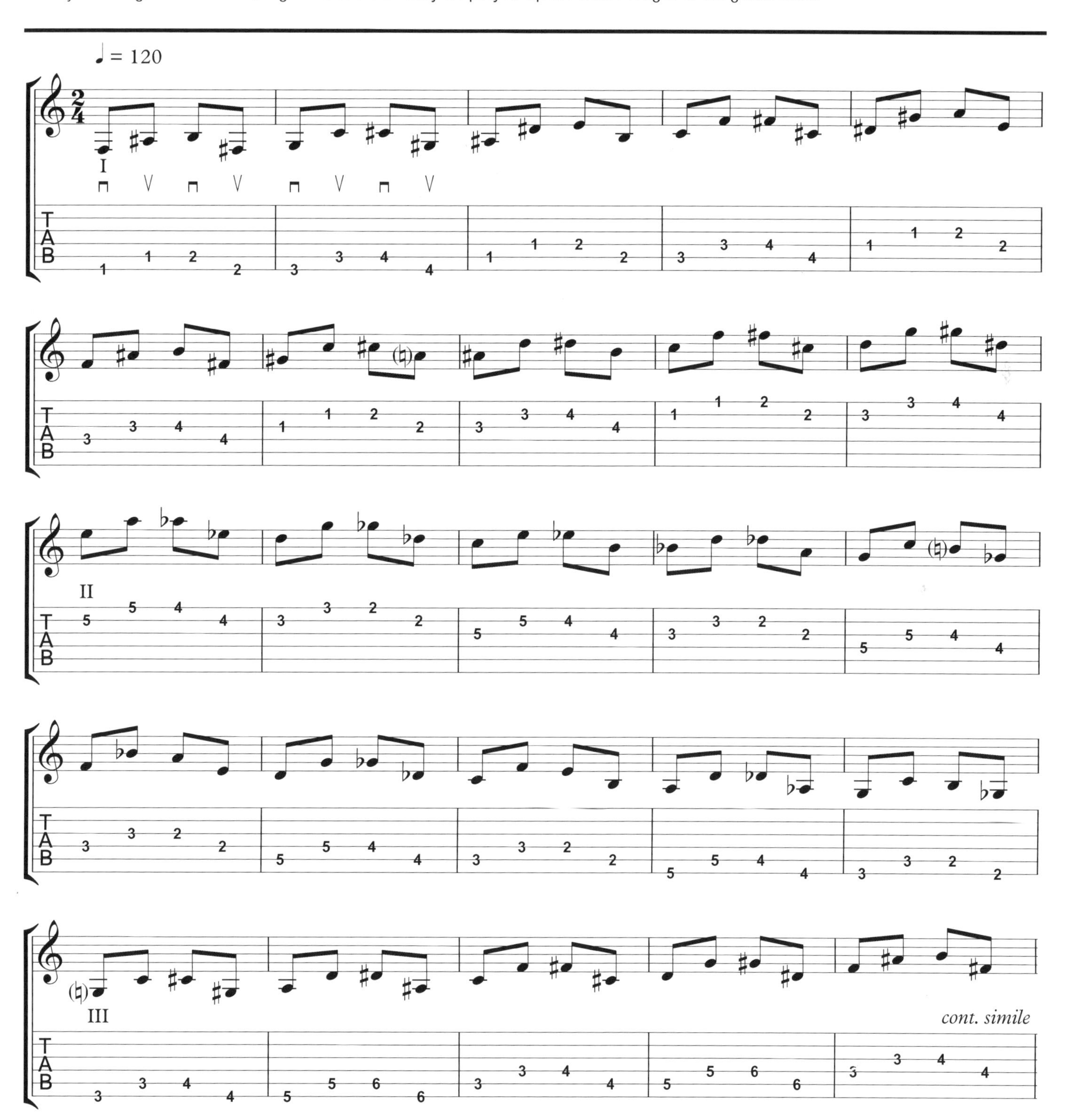

DATE OF COMPLETION: ____________________

LEVEL 2: EXERCISE 42

This exercise combines alternate picking, string switching and finger rolls, using the finger pattern 1-3-2-4. Upon completing the finger pattern on the B-string and high E-string, move up to second position and play the reverse finger pattern from the B-string. Use alternate picking throughout, and continue to roll your fingers to the adjacent higher or lower string. This exercise may be played up the entire length of the guitar neck.

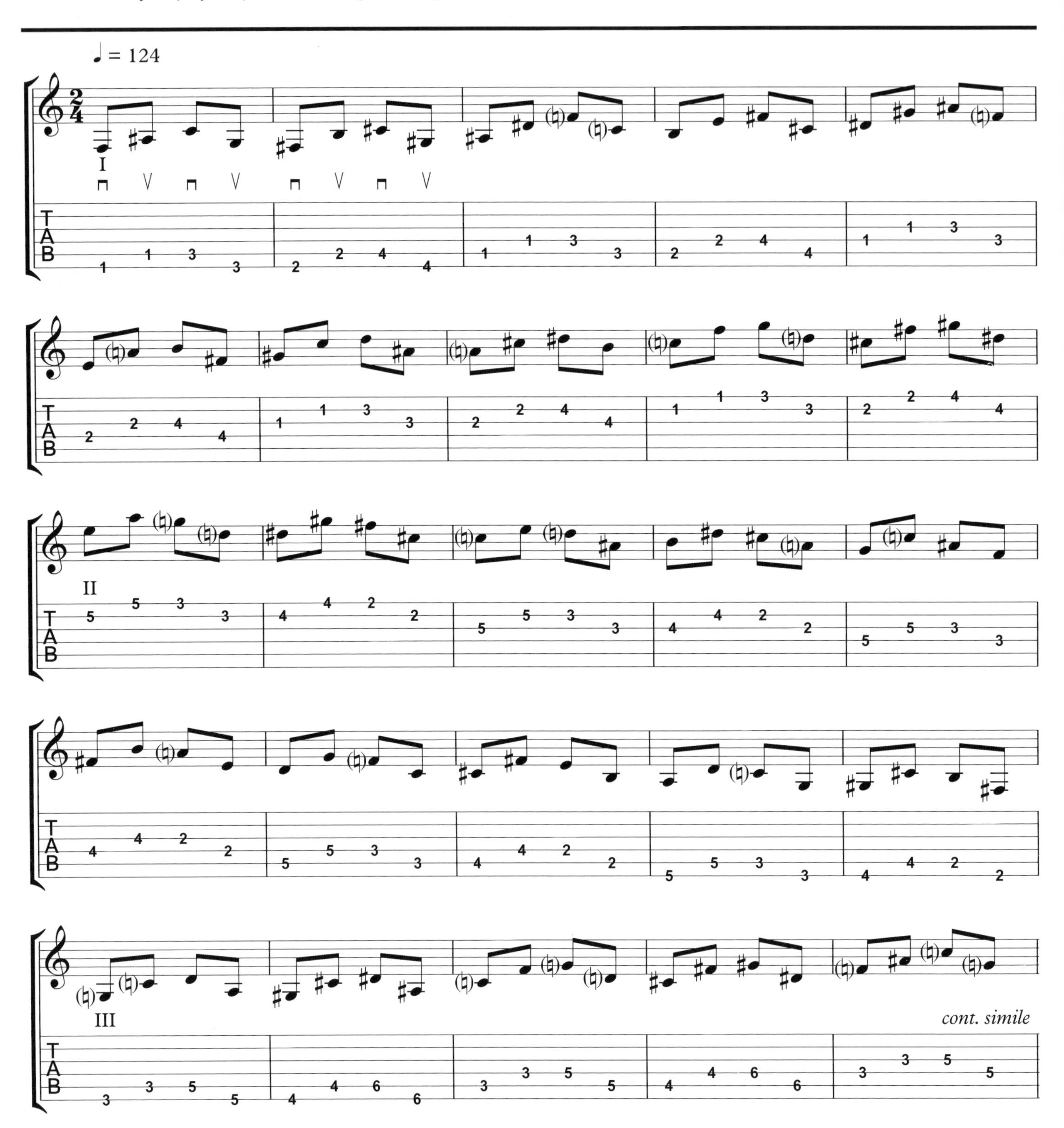

DATE OF COMPLETION: ______________________

LEVEL 2: EXERCISE 43

All eighth note slide exercises thus far have been written so that the note preceding the legato slides begins on a beat, requiring a downstroke as the picking method. However, the note preceding the slides may also begin in between the beats, requiring you to pick with an upstroke. Pay careful attention to the picking in this exercise, as you will have to pick two upstrokes in a row – one preceding the slide and one following the slide. Upon completing the slide sequence on the high E-string, move up to second position and play the pattern again from the high E-string. This exercise may be played up the entire length of the guitar neck.

DATE OF COMPLETION: ______________________________

LEVEL 2: EXERCISE 44

Like the previous slide exercise, hammer-ons may also require a preceding upstroke. For this exercise, alternate the finger patterns 4-2-3-1 and 1-2-3-4, using a hammer-on from finger 2 to 3 and rolling the first and fourth finger to adjacent strings. Be sure to pick two upstrokes in a row – one preceding the hammer-on and one following it. Before completing the hammer-on sequence on the high E-string, replace the last hammer-on with an upward slide into second position and play the pattern again from the high E-string. This exercise may be played up the entire length of the guitar neck.

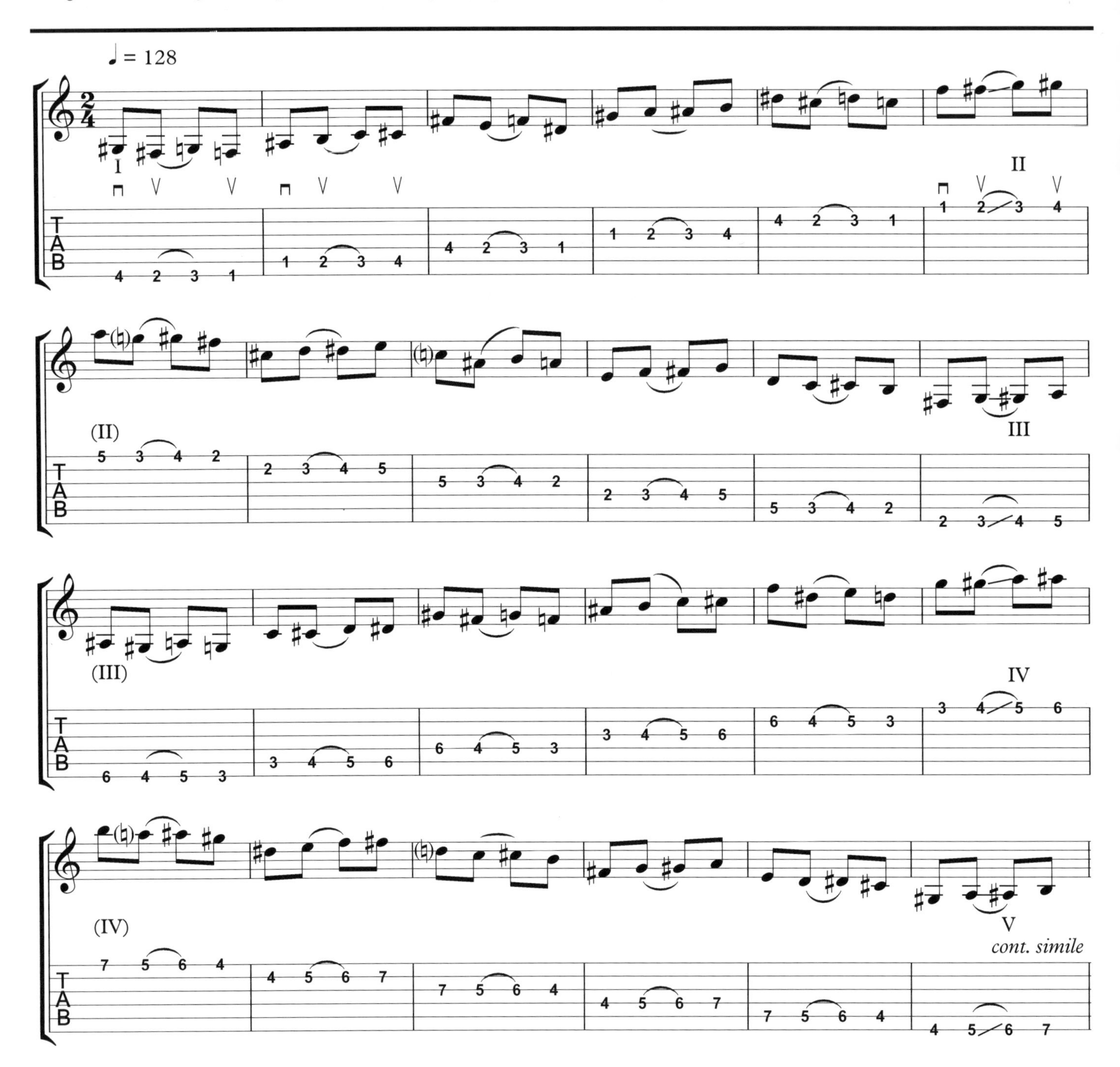

DATE OF COMPLETION: ______________________

LEVEL 2: EXERCISE 45

Similar to the previous exercise, this exercise will show how to play pull-offs with a preceding upstroke. Alternate the finger patterns 4-3-2-1 and 1-3-2-4, using a pull-off from finger 3 to 2 and rolling the first and fourth finger to adjacent strings. Be sure to pick two upstrokes in a row – one preceding the pull-off and one following it. Before completing the pull-off sequence on the high E-string, replace the last pull-off with an upward slide into second position and play the pattern again from the high E-string. This exercise may be played up the entire length of the guitar neck.

DATE OF COMPLETION: ____________________

LEVEL 2: EXERCISE 46

This exercise combines legato slides, hammer-ons and pull-offs, all with preceding and following upstrokes. Alternate the finger patterns 4-2-3-1 and 1-3-2-4, using a hammer-on or pull-off mid-measure, and rolling the first and fourth finger to adjacent strings. Before completing the sequence on the high E-string, replace the last pull-off with an upward slide into second position and play the pattern again from the high E-string. This exercise may be played up the entire length of the guitar neck.

DATE OF COMPLETION: ______________________

LEVEL 2: EXERCISE 47

This exercise will focus on string skipping and alternate picking, with the finger pattern 1-3-4-2 played twice on each set of strings. Before completing the finger pattern in first position, replace the last measure with an upward slide into second position and play the finger pattern again from the high E-string. Follow the picking closely for this measure, as it contains two consecutive upstrokes: one preceding and one following the slide. This exercise may be played up the entire length of the guitar neck.

DATE OF COMPLETION: ______________________

MUSIC NOTATION: TRIPLETS

A *triplet* is a group of three notes having the same combined time value as two notes of the same type. For example, in a 4/4 time signature, two eighth notes have the combined value of one beat. Likewise, in the same time signature, three eighth note triplets have the combined value of one beat. Eighth note triplets are notated with a beam connecting all three notes and a number "3" next to the beam.

Eighth note triplets are represented as

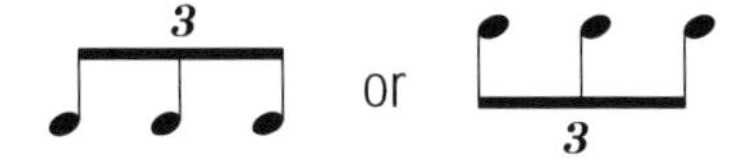

COUNTING EIGHTH NOTE TRIPLETS

The best system to use for counting triplets is by using "tri-pl-et," as a three syllable word. If one of the notes in a triplet rhythm is on a beat, then replace the "tri" with the beat number. For example, a triplet at the start of a measure should be counted as "1-pl-et." Below are two examples of the appropriate method that should be used for counting eighth note triplets. Make sure to keep a steady beat, or for best results count with a metronome.

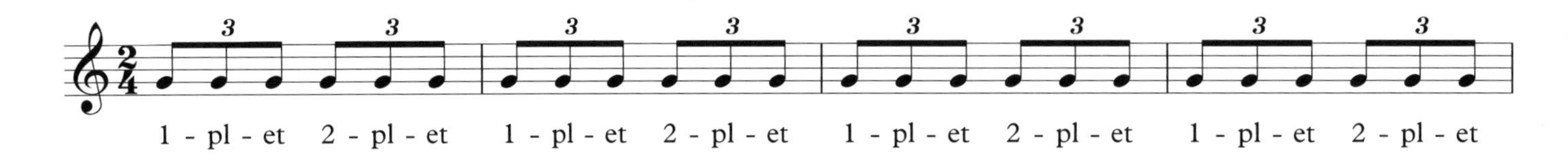

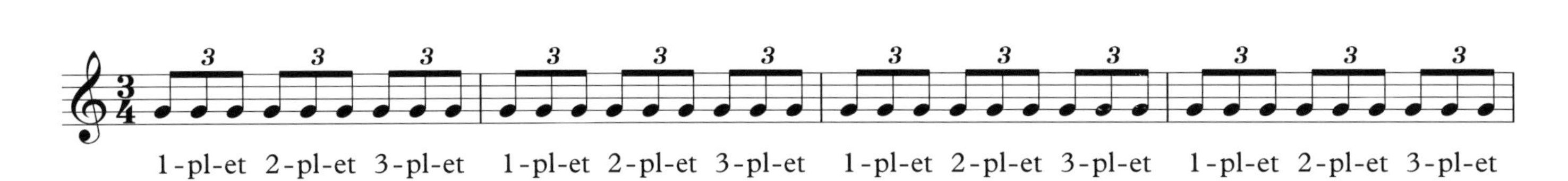

LEVEL 2: EXERCISE 48

To prepare yourself for the upcoming eighth note triplet exercises, you should first train your picking hand. Eighth note triplets should be played with strict alternate picking, which will sometimes cause your hand to pick upward on a beat. This will feel a bit backwards at first, but steady practice will allow you to absorb this method. For this exercise, pick six times on each string, playing two groups of triplets. This exercise may be played in repetition by playing from the last measure to the first measure without a break.

DATE OF COMPLETION: ______________________

LEVEL 2: EXERCISE 49

For this exercise, pick three eighth note triplets on each string before switching to the adjacent higher or lower string. Continue to use strict alternate picking, constantly alternating downstrokes and upstrokes. This exercise may be played in repetition by playing from the last measure to the first measure without a break.

DATE OF COMPLETION: ______________________

LEVEL 2: EXERCISE 50

Using the finger patterns 1-2-3-1-2-3 and 4-3-2-4-3-2, play two sets of eighth note triplets per string. Alternate the finger patterns when switching strings, and be sure to constantly use alternate picking. Before completing the finger pattern in first position, replace the last triplet with the finger pattern 4-3-1, move up to second position and play the pattern again from the high E-string. This exercise may be played up the entire length of the guitar neck.

DATE OF COMPLETION: ______________________

LEVEL 2: EXERCISE 51

Using the finger pattern 1-2-3-4-3-2, play two sets of eighth note triplets per string. Before completing the finger pattern in first position, replace the last triplet with the finger pattern 2-3-4, move up to second position and play the reverse finger pattern from the high E-string. This exercise may be played up the entire length of the guitar neck.

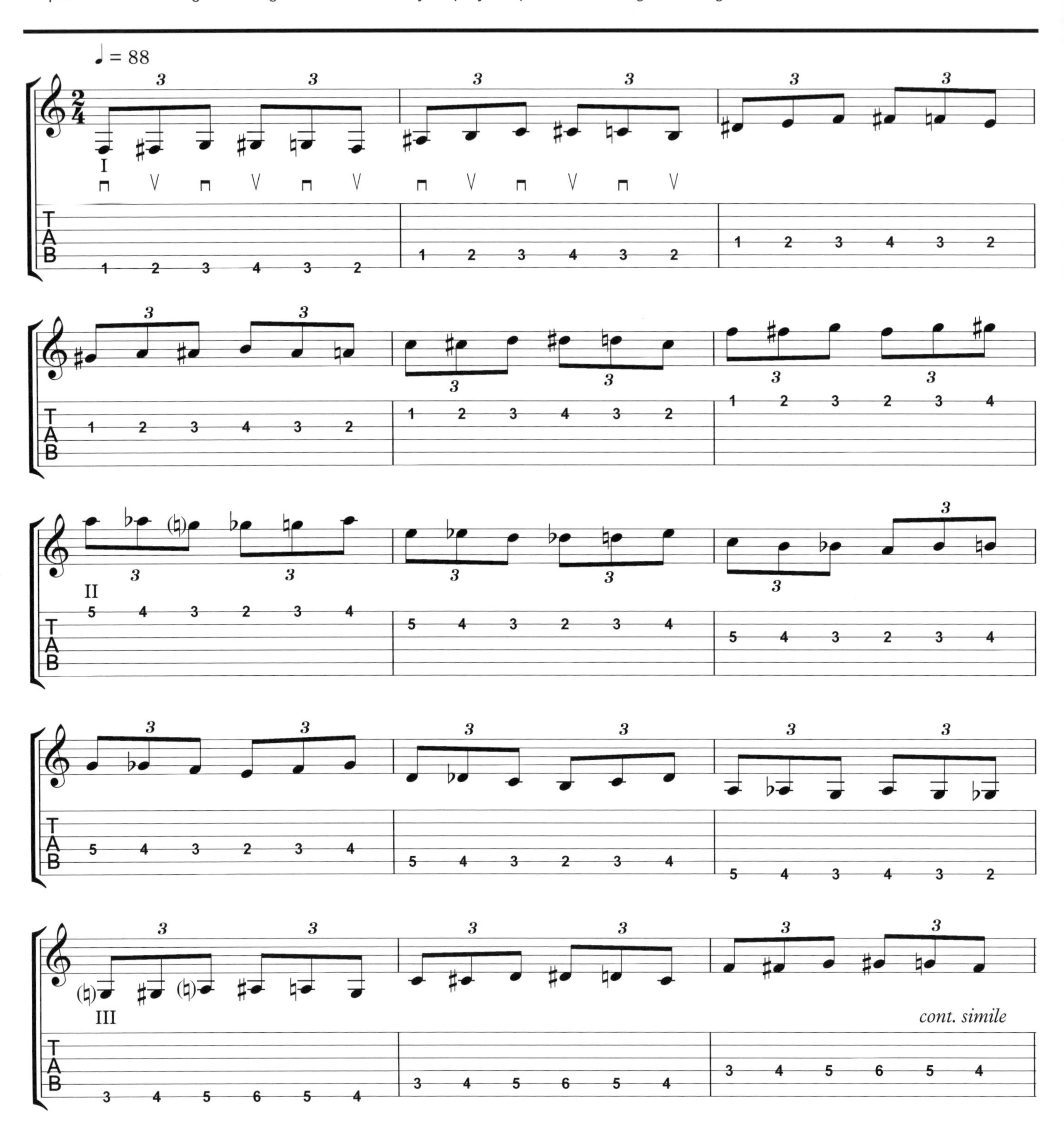

DATE OF COMPLETION: ______________________

LEVEL 3: EXERCISE 52

This exercise will focus on combining alternate picking with string switching while playing eighth note triplets. Upon completing the finger pattern in first position, move up to second position and play the reverse finger pattern from the high E-string. This exercise may be played up the entire length of the guitar neck.

DATE OF COMPLETION: ____________________

LEVEL 3: EXERCISE 53

This exercise will include a combination of alternate picking, string switching and finger rolls. Be sure to use strict alternate picking the entire time, and roll your finger mid-measure to switch strings. Upon completing the exercise in first position, move up to second position and play the reverse finger pattern from the high E-string. This exercise may be played up the entire length of the guitar neck.

DATE OF COMPLETION: ______________________

MUSIC NOTATION: SIXTEENTH NOTES

Sixteenth notes are half the value of eighth notes, which means that a sixteenth note will receive one fourth of a beat in a 2/4, 3/4 or 4/4 time signature. These notes will allow for even more speed, as the notes are twice as fast as eighth notes. In standard music notation, sixteenth notes will often times be grouped together by use of a double beam.

Sixteenth notes may be represented as

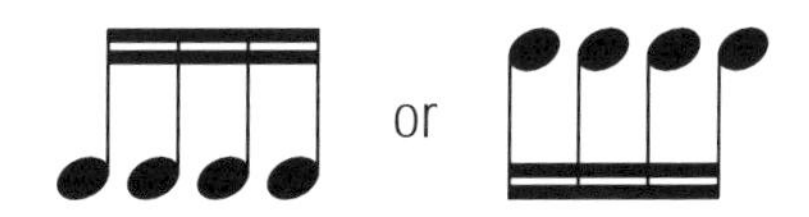

COUNTING SIXTEENTH NOTES

The best system to use for counting sixteenth notes is by using a beat number followed by "e-&-a" to cover all four sixteenth notes. For example, a group of sixteenth notes at the start of a measure should be counted as "1-e-&-a." Below are two examples of the appropriate method that should be used for counting sixteenth notes. Make sure to keep a steady beat, or for best results count with a metronome.

DATE OF COMPLETION: ______________________

LEVEL 3: EXERCISE 54

To prepare yourself for the following sixteenth note exercises, you should first train your picking hand. Sixteenth notes should be played two times as fast as eighth notes, and should use alternate picking that moves two times as fast. Therefore, you should use a downstroke on each beat and mid-way in between each beat, on the "&." Upstrokes should be used in between each downstroke. For this exercise, pick eight times on each string before switching to an adjacent higher or lower string. This exercise may be played in repetition by playing from the last measure to the first measure without a break.

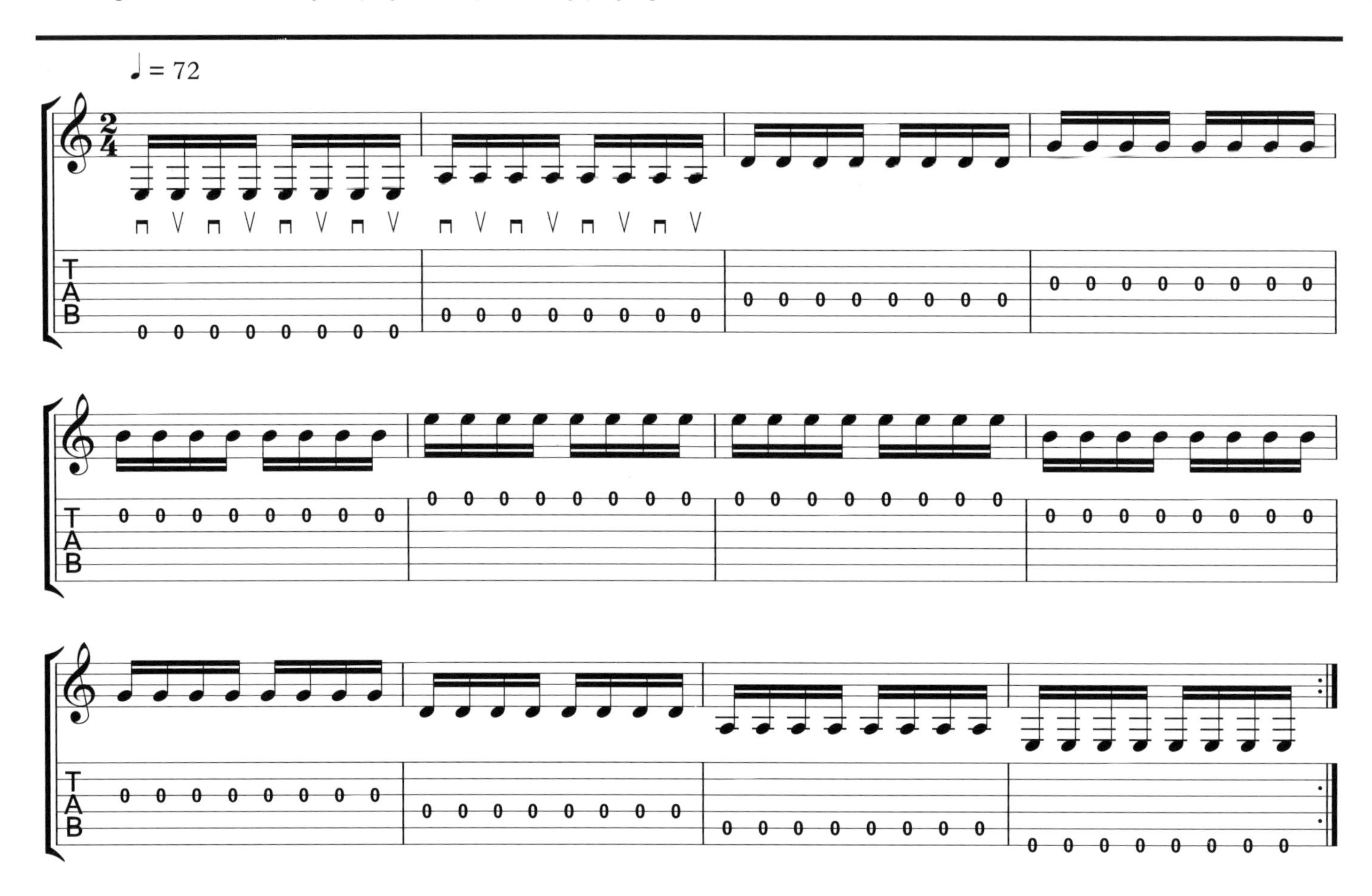

DATE OF COMPLETION: ______________________

LEVEL 3: EXERCISE 55

For this exercise, pick four sixteenth notes on each string before switching to the adjacent higher or lower string. Be sure to constantly alternate downstrokes and upstrokes the entire time. This exercise may be played in repetition by playing from the last measure to the first measure without a break.

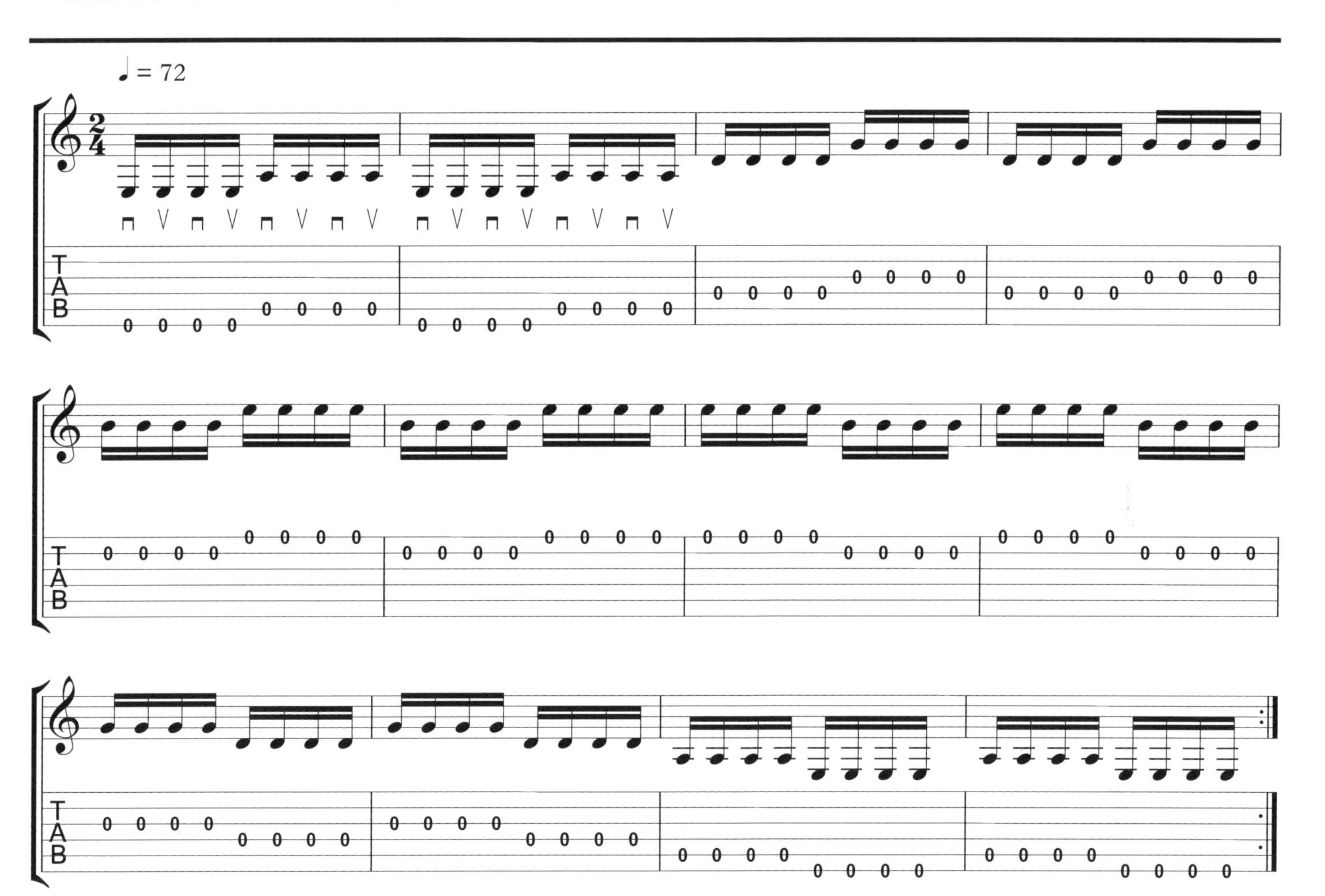

DATE OF COMPLETION: ______________________________

LEVEL 3: EXERCISE 56

Using the finger patterns 1-2-3-4 and 1-3-2-4, play eight sixteenth notes per string. When switching strings, be sure to roll your finger and then play the reverse finger patterns. Upon completing the finger pattern in first position, move up to second position and play the pattern again from the high E-string. This exercise may be played up the entire length of the guitar neck.

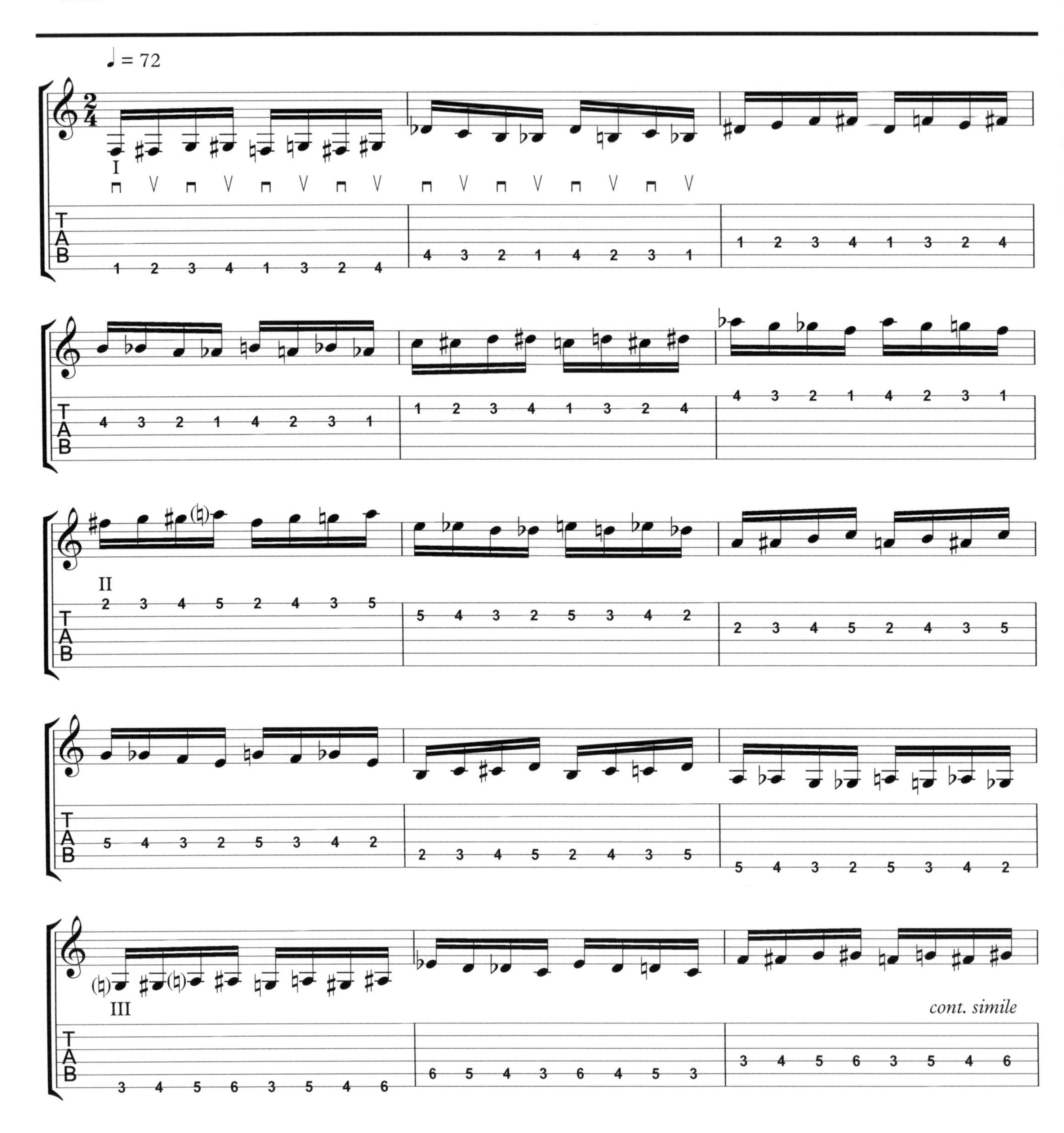

DATE OF COMPLETION: ________________________

LEVEL 3: EXERCISE 57

While using the same finger patterns as the previous exercise, play four sixteenth notes per string before rolling your finger and playing the reverse finger pattern on an adjacent string. Upon completing the finger pattern in first position, move up to second position and play the pattern again from the high E-string. This exercise may be played up the entire length of the guitar neck.

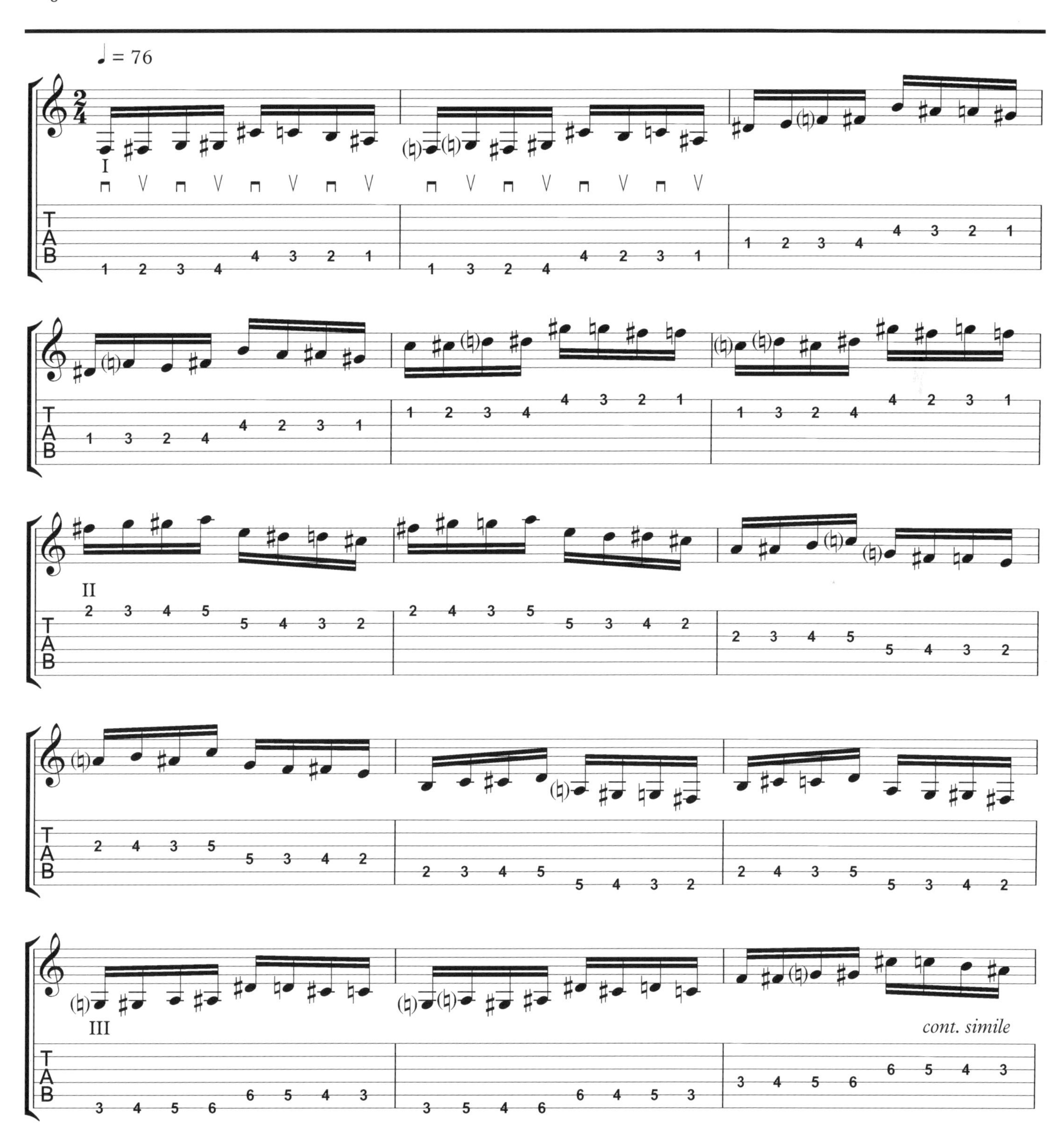

DATE OF COMPLETION: ____________________

LEVEL 3: EXERCISE 58

This exercise will include a combination of legato slides, string switching and finger rolls with eighth note triplets. Because the middle note of each triplet is a slide, you can use a different picking system: use a downstroke before each slide and an upstroke following each slide. Before completing the slide pattern on the B-string and high E-string, remove the slides from the last measure and pick every note. Then, repeat the slide pattern again starting from the high E-string in second position. This pattern may be played up the entire length of the guitar neck.

DATE OF COMPLETION: ____________________

LEVEL 3: EXERCISE 59

This exercise will focus on a combination of hammer-ons, pull-offs and string switching with eighth note triplets. Because the middle note of each triplet is either a hammer-on or a pull-off, you can use a similar picking system to the previous slide exercise: use a downstroke before and an upstroke following each hammer-on/pull-off. Before completing the pattern in first position, use a legato slide on the high E-string to move into second position and then repeat the reverse finger pattern. This pattern may be played up the entire length of the guitar neck.

LEVEL 3: EXERCISE 60

Using the finger patterns 1-3-2-4 and 4-2-3-1, play two sixteenth notes on each string before switching to the adjacent higher or lower string. Be sure to use alternate picking the entire time. Upon completing the finger pattern in first position, move up to second position and play the pattern again from the high E-string. This exercise may be played up the entire length of the guitar neck.

DATE OF COMPLETION: ______________________

LEVEL 3: EXERCISE 61

This eighth note triplet exercise will use the finger patterns 1-2-3 and 4-3-2 to focus on string skipping and alternate picking. Before completing the pattern in first position, replace the last finger pattern with 4-3-1 so that you may move into second position and play the finger pattern again from the high E-string. This exercise may be played up the entire length of the guitar neck.

DATE OF COMPLETION: ______________________

LEVEL 3: EXERCISE 62

This exercise will focus on a combination of legato slides and string switching with sixteenth notes. Starting in first position, be sure to follow each slide with two picked notes on an adjacent string. Before completing this pattern on the B-string and high E-string, replace the last downward slide with an upward slide into third position and begin a reverse pattern from the high E-string. This reverse pattern will include picking two notes before sliding on an adjacent string. This exercise may be played up the entire length of the guitar neck.

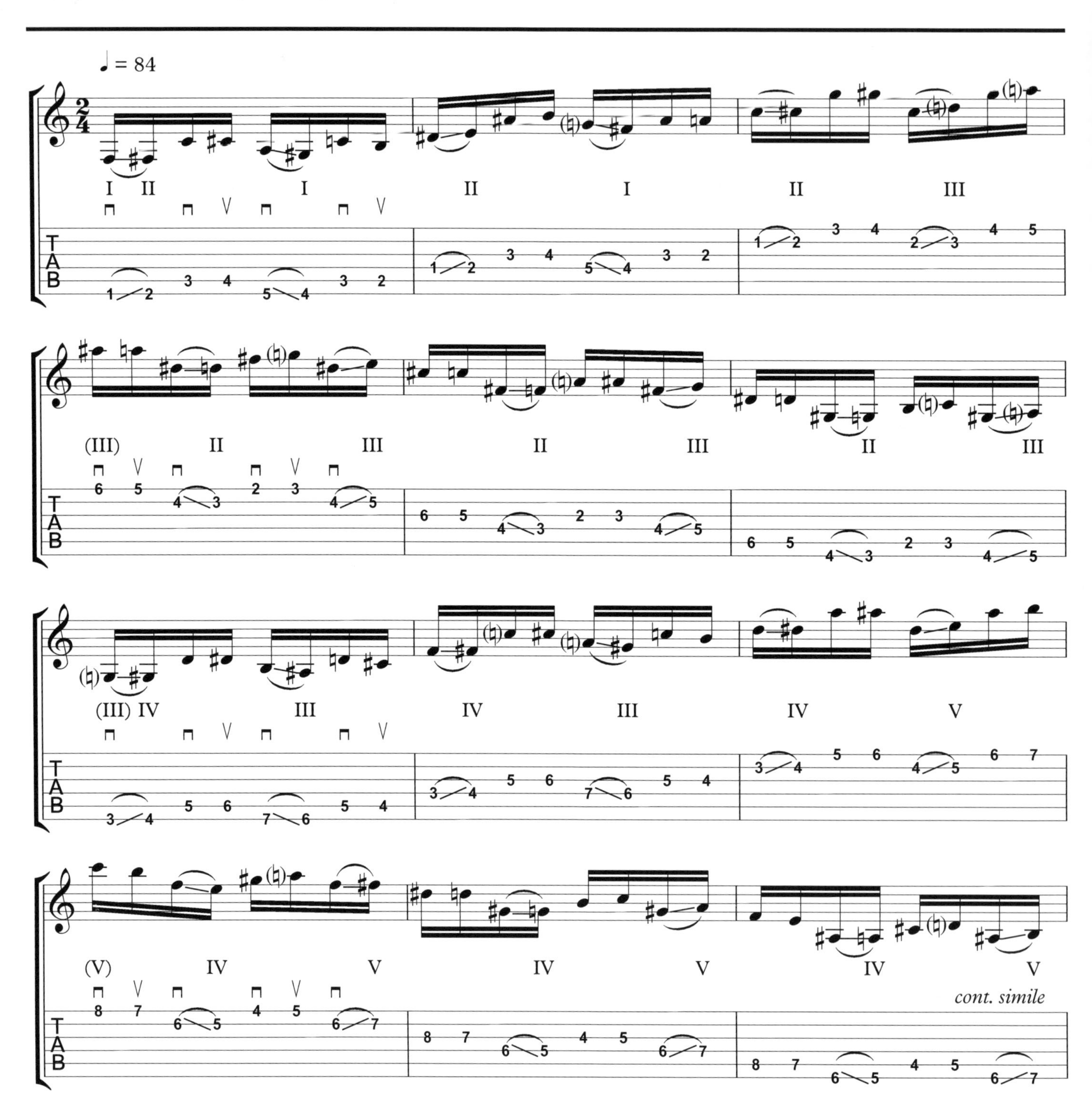

DATE OF COMPLETION: ____________________

LEVEL 3: EXERCISE 63

This exercise will focus on a combination of hammer-ons, pull-offs and string switching with sixteenth notes. Before completing the pattern on the B-string and high E-string, replace the last hammer-on with an upward slide into second position and play the reverse finger pattern from the high E-string. This exercise may be played up the entire length of the guitar neck.

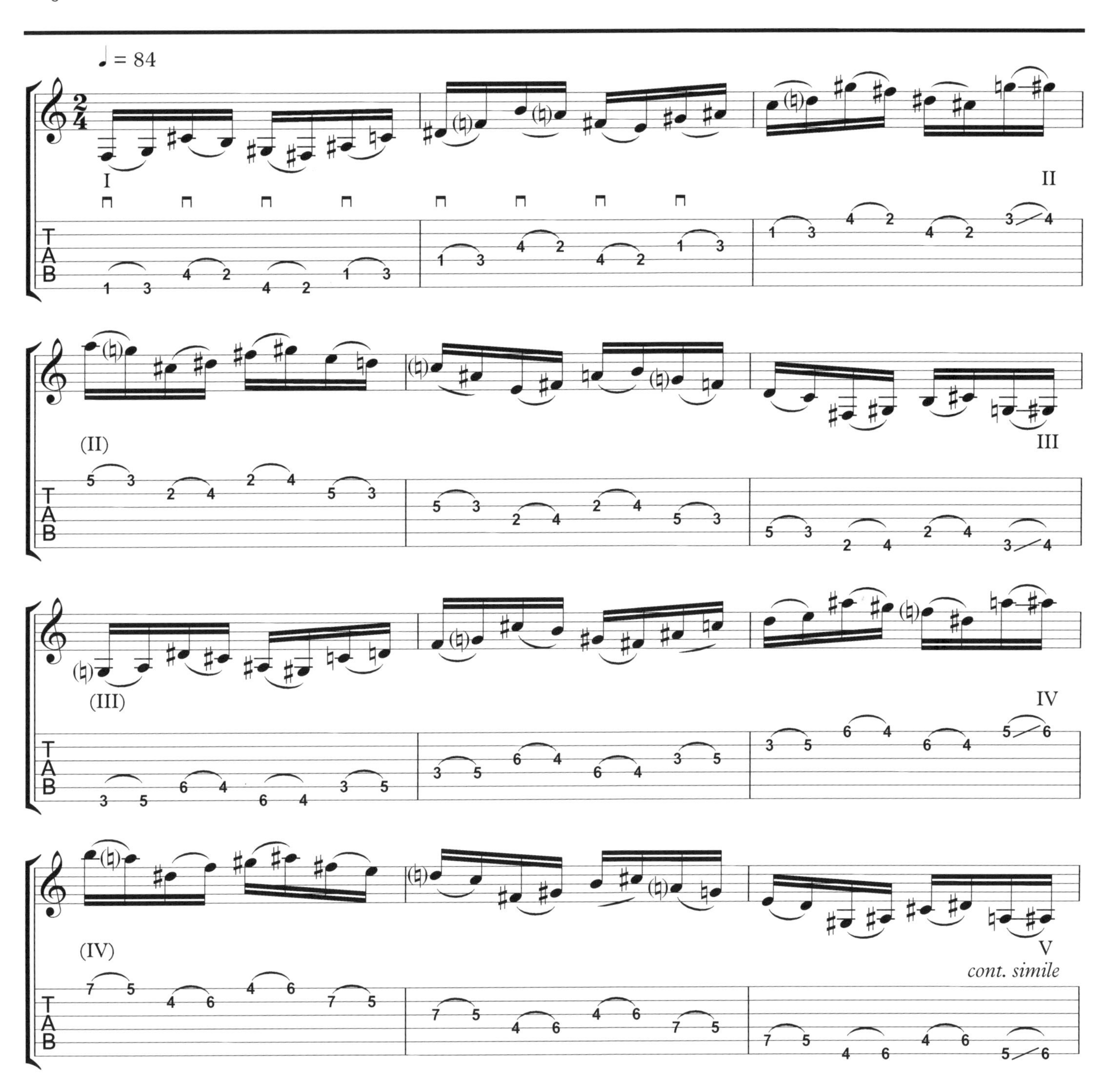

DATE OF COMPLETION: ______________________

LEVEL 3: EXERCISE 64

When playing eighth note triplets, it is sometimes necessary to switch strings within a triplet group. To train your picking hand to continuously use alternate picking in these instances, pick each string four times before switching to the adjacent higher or lower string. Pay careful attention that you are using alternate picking the entire time. This exercise may be played in repetition by playing from the last measure to the first measure without a break.

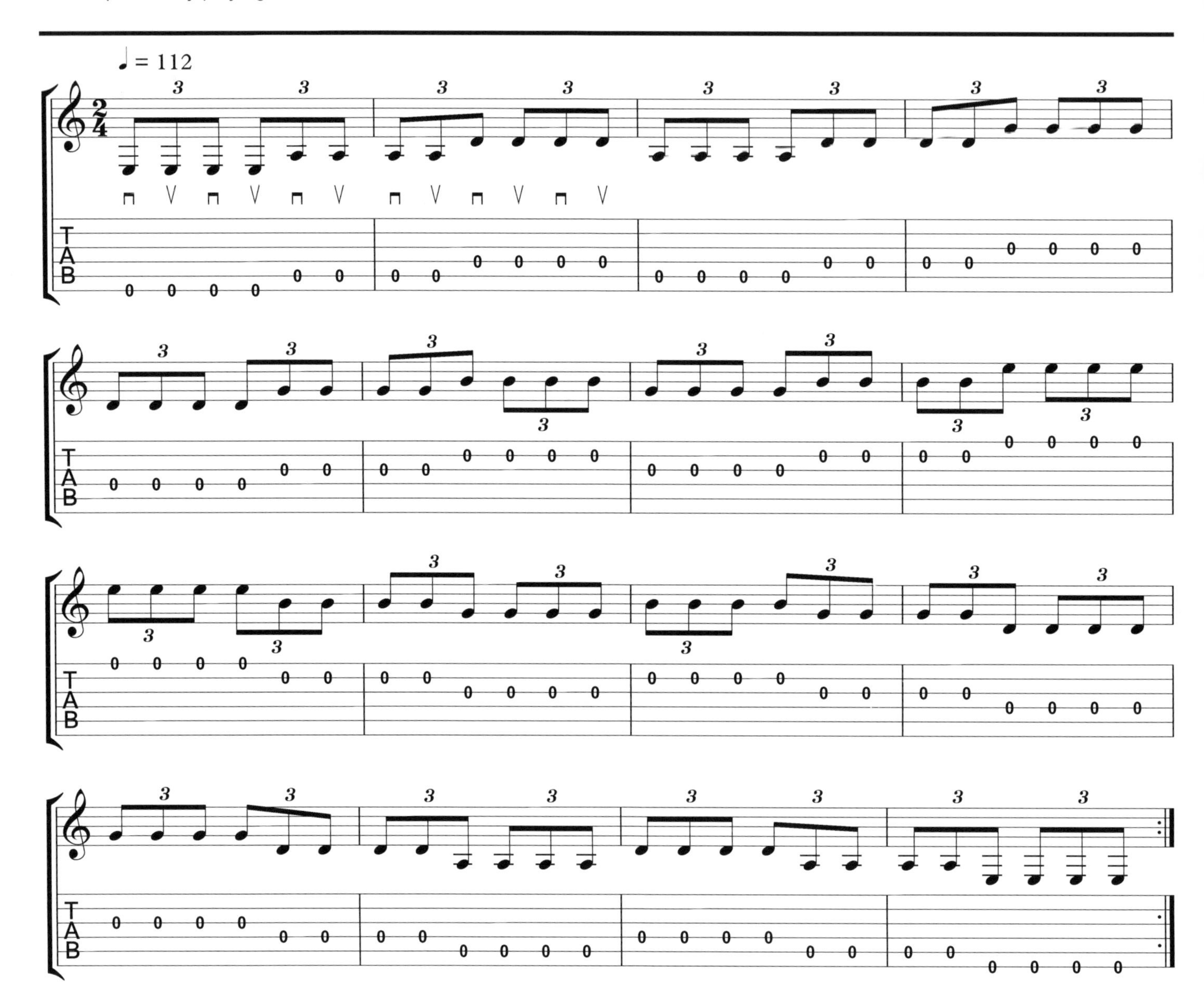

DATE OF COMPLETION: ______________________

LEVEL 3: EXERCISE 65

For this eighth note triplet picking exercise, pick each string two times before switching to the adjacent higher or lower string. Pay careful attention that you are using alternate picking the entire time. This exercise may be played in repetition by playing from the last measure to the first measure without a break.

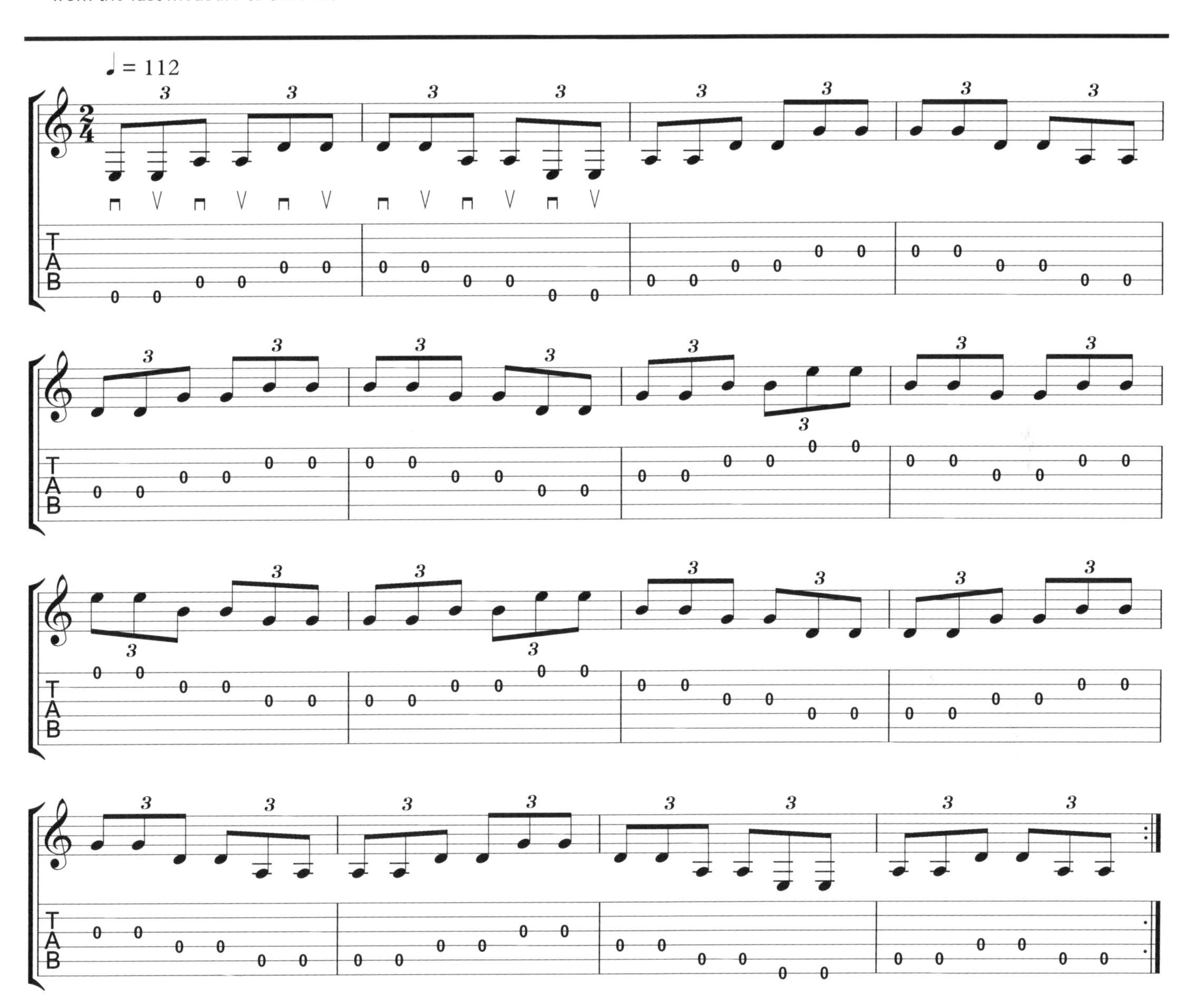

LEVEL 3: EXERCISE 66

Using the finger patterns 1-2-3-4 and 4-3-2-1, play four eighth note triplets per string. When switching strings, be sure to roll your finger and then play the reverse finger pattern. Upon completing the finger pattern in first position, move up to second position and play the pattern again from the high E-string. This exercise may be played up the entire length of the guitar neck.

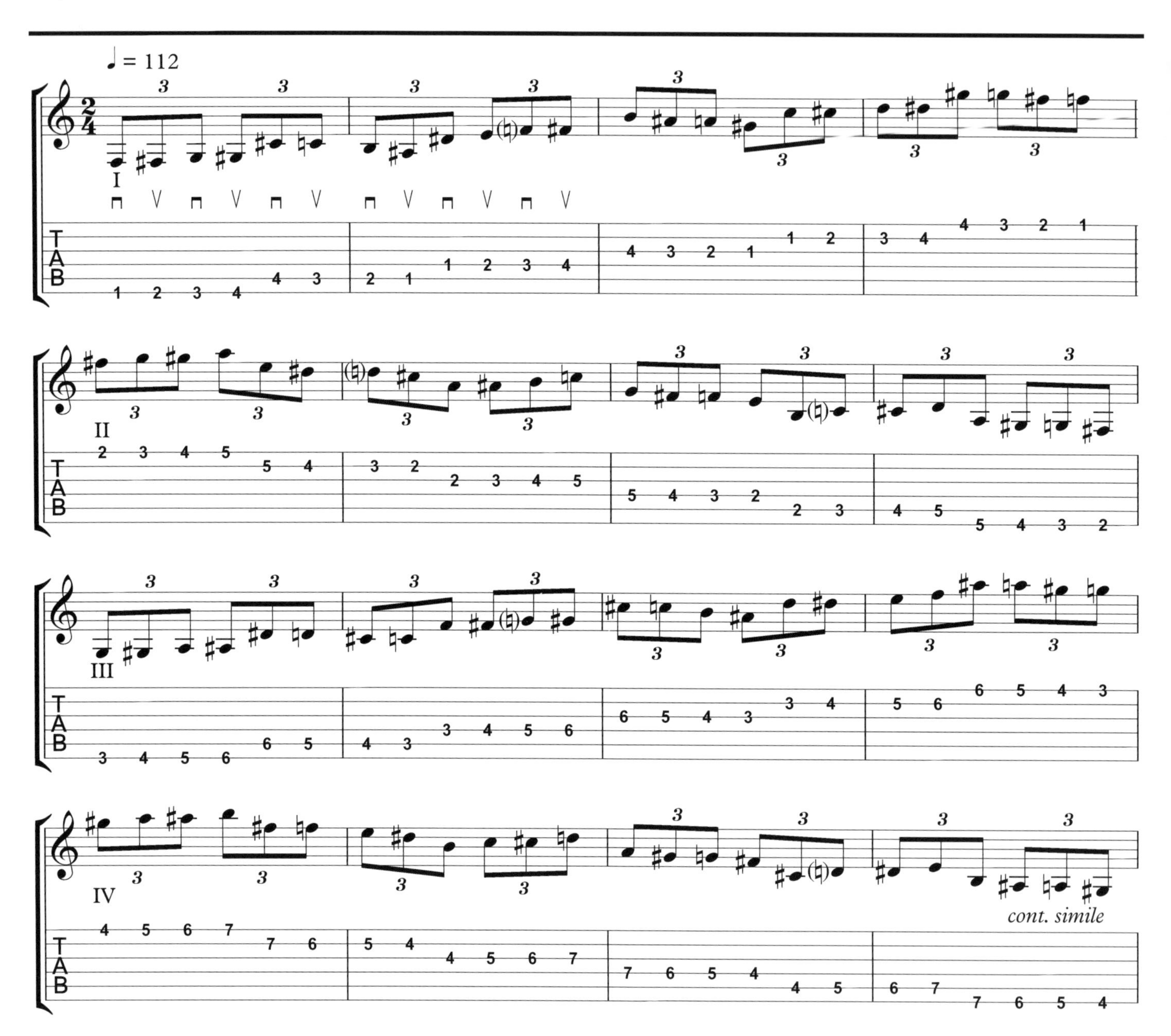

DATE OF COMPLETION: ______________________

LEVEL 3: EXERCISE 67

Using the finger patterns 1-3-2-4 and 4-2-3-1, play four eighth note triplets per string before switching to an adjacent higher or lower string. When switching strings, be sure to roll your finger and then play the reverse finger pattern. Upon completing the finger pattern in first position, move up to second position and play the pattern again from the high E-string. This exercise may be played up the entire length of the guitar neck.

LEVEL 3: EXERCISE 68

This exercise will focus on string skipping with sixteenth notes, using the finger patterns 1-3-2-4 and 4-2-3-1. Always be sure to roll your 1st or 4th finger when switching to an adjacent string. Before completing the pattern in first position, use a legato slide on the high E-string to move into second position and play the pattern again from the high E-string. This exercise may be played up the entire length of the guitar neck.

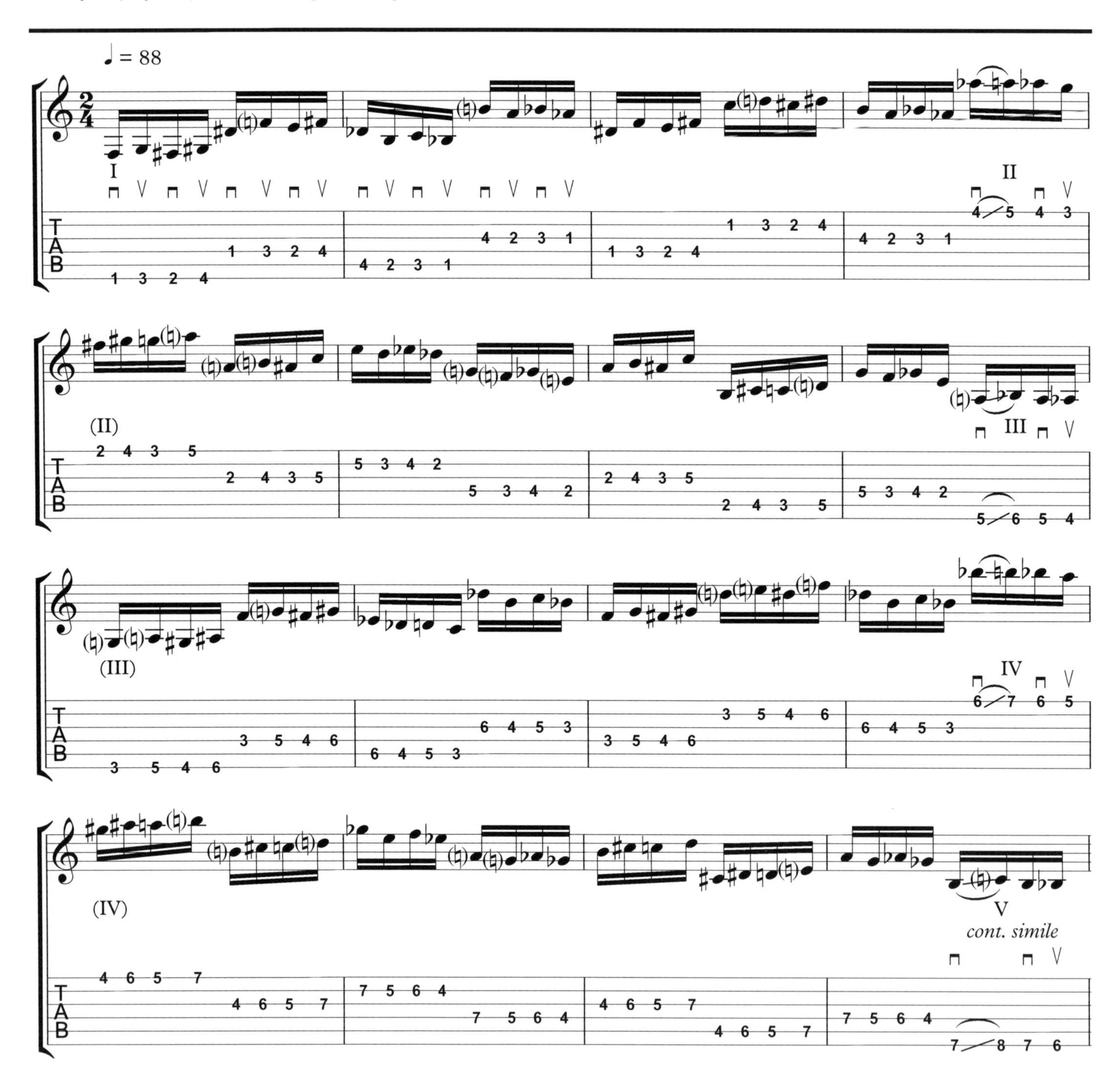

DATE OF COMPLETION: ______________________

LEVEL 3: EXERCISE 69

This exercise combines alternate picking, string switching and finger rolls with eighth note triplets, using the finger patterns 1-2-3-4 and 4-3-2-1. Upon completing the finger pattern on the B-string and high E-string, move up to second position and play the finger pattern again from the high E-string. Pay careful attention that you are using alternate picking the entire time, and that your fingers always roll to the adjacent higher or lower string. This exercise may be played up the entire length of the guitar neck.

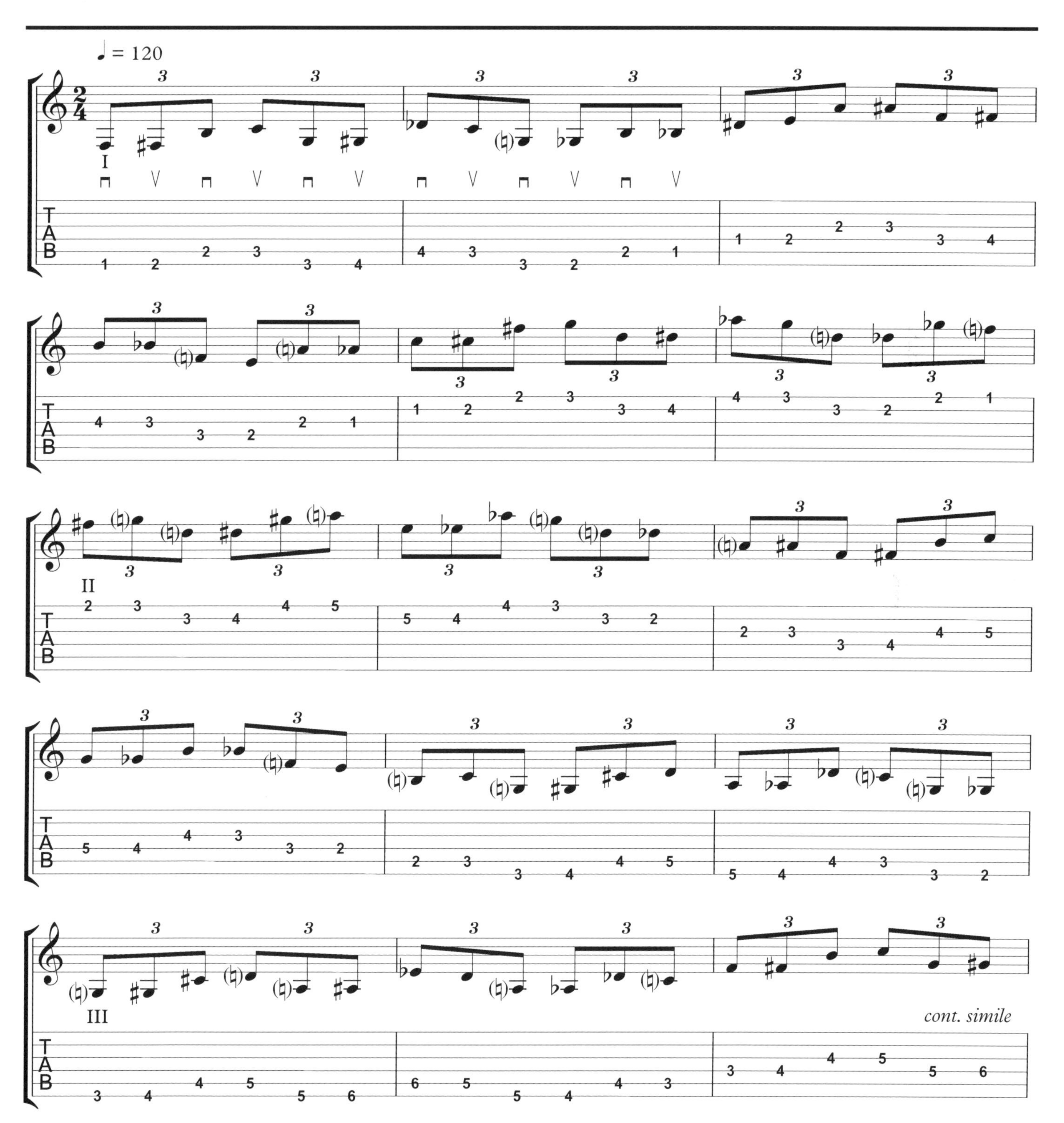

DATE OF COMPLETION: ____________________

LEVEL 3: EXERCISE 70

When playing sixteenth notes, it is sometimes necessary to switch strings on an upstroke. To train your picking hand to continuously use alternate picking in these instances, pick each string three times before switching to the adjacent higher or lower string. Pay careful attention that you are using alternate picking the entire time. This exercise may be played in repetition by playing from the last measure to the first measure without a break.

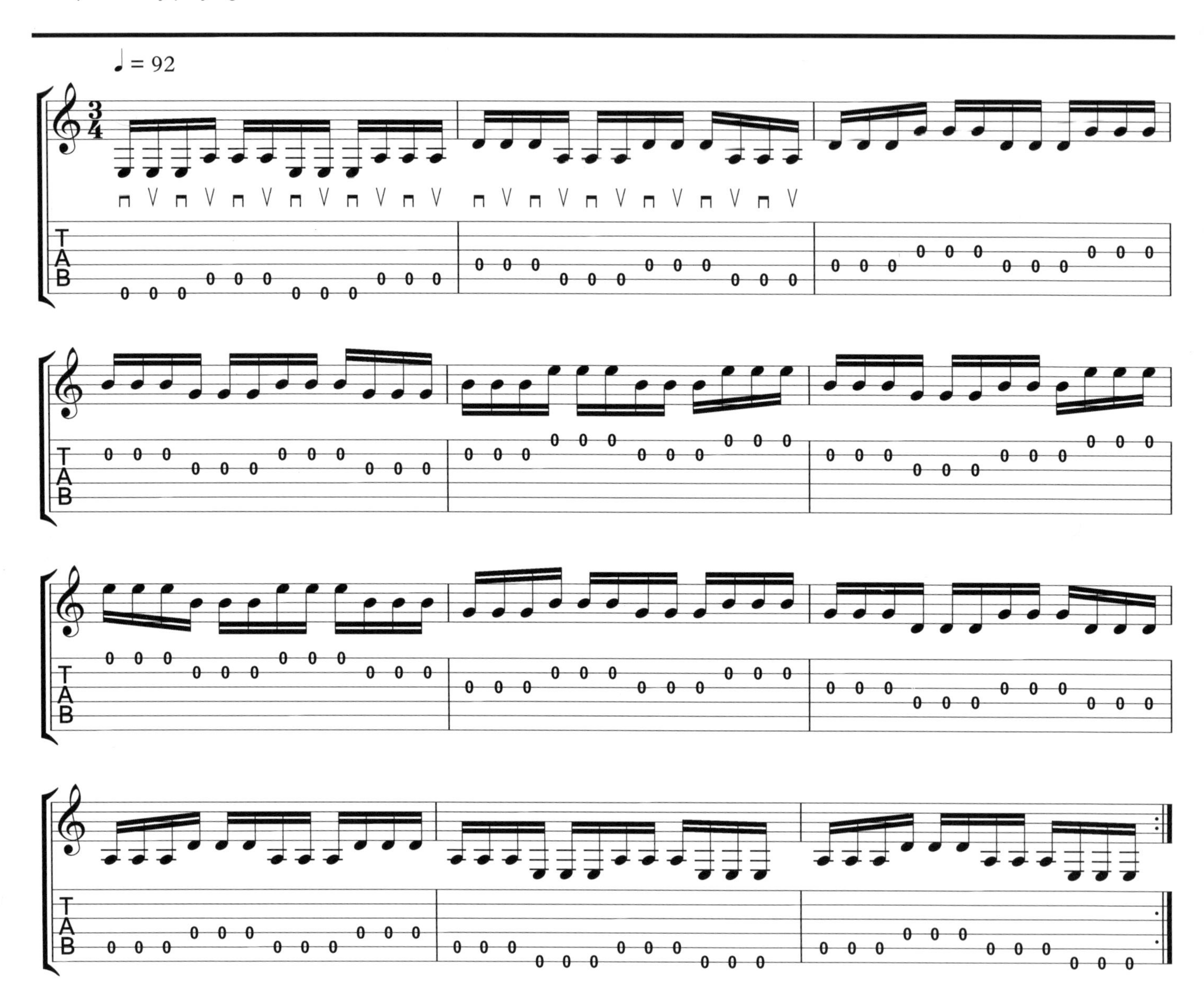

DATE OF COMPLETION: ______________________

LEVEL 3: EXERCISE 71

Using the finger patterns 1-2-3, 2-3-4, 4-3-2 and 3-2-1, play three sixteenth notes per string before switching to an adjacent higher or lower string. This will sometimes involve rolling your 1st or 4th finger to an adjacent string. Before completing the pattern in first position, use a legato slide on the high E-string to move into second position and play the reverse finger pattern from the high E-string. Pay careful attention that you are using alternate picking the entire time. This exercise may be played up the entire length of the guitar neck.

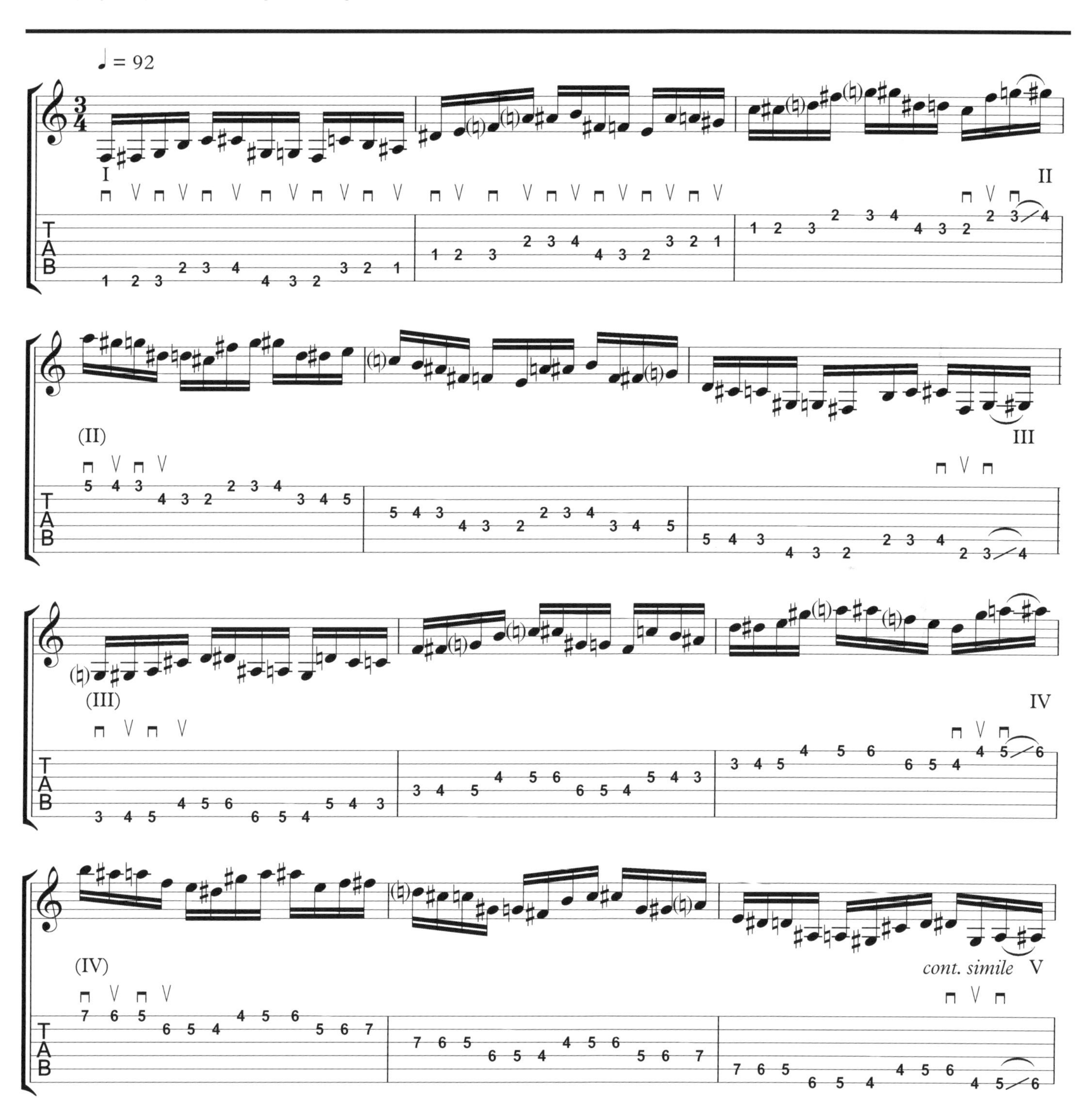

DATE OF COMPLETION: ______________________

LEVEL 3: EXERCISE 72

This exercise combines string switching with finger rolls, using eighth note triplets. Upon completing the pattern in first position, move up to second position and play the pattern again from the high E-string. Be sure to always roll your finger to an adjacent string and to use alternate picking the entire time. This exercise may be played up the entire length of the guitar neck.

DATE OF COMPLETION: ______________________

LEVEL 3: EXERCISE 73

This exercise will combine alternate picking with very frequent string switching of sixteenth notes, using the finger pattern 1-3-4-2. Before completing the finger pattern on the B-string and high E-string, use a legato slide on the high E-string to move into second position and play the reverse finger pattern from the high E-string. Pay careful attention that you are using alternate picking the entire time. This exercise may be played up the entire length of the guitar neck.

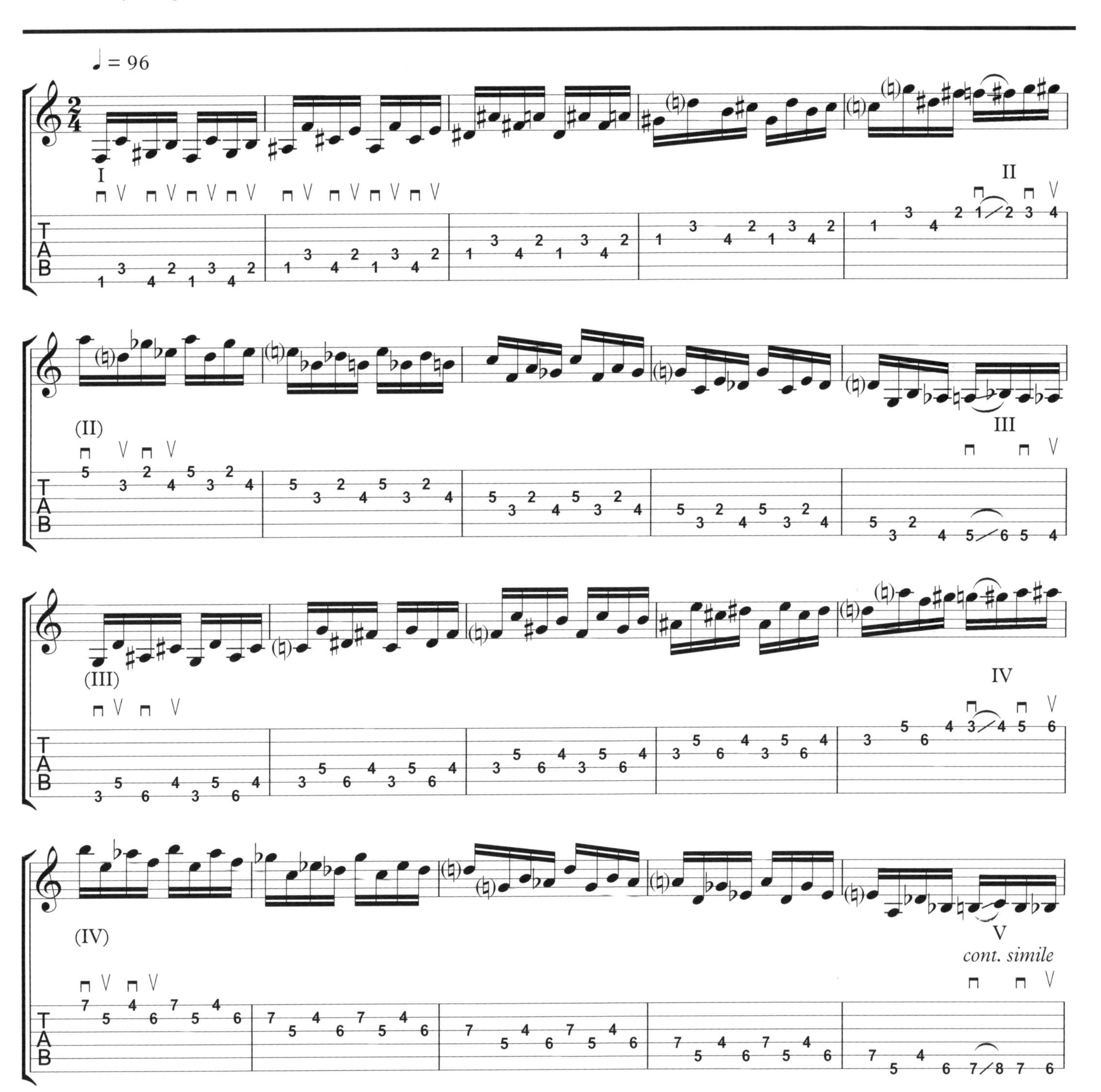

DATE OF COMPLETION: ______________________

LEVEL 3: EXERCISE 74

This exercise will include a combination of legato slides and string switching with eighth note triplets. Because the middle note of each triplet is a slide, you can use a downstroke before each slide and an upstroke following each slide. Before completing the slide pattern on the B-string and high E-string, replace the last downward slide with an upward slide into third position and repeat the slide pattern in reverse. This exercise may be played up the entire length of the guitar neck.

DATE OF COMPLETION: ______________________________

LEVEL 3: EXERCISE 75

This exercise will focus on a technique of combined hammer-ons and pull-offs, using eighth note triplets. Each triplet will either be 1) a hammer-on followed by an immediate pull-off or 2) a pull-off followed by an immediate hammer-on. The first note of each triplet should be picked, and the remaining notes should be played by use of hammer-ons or pull-offs. Before completing the pattern in first position, use a legato slide on the high E-string to move into second position and then repeat the reverse finger pattern. This exercise may be played up the entire length of the guitar neck.

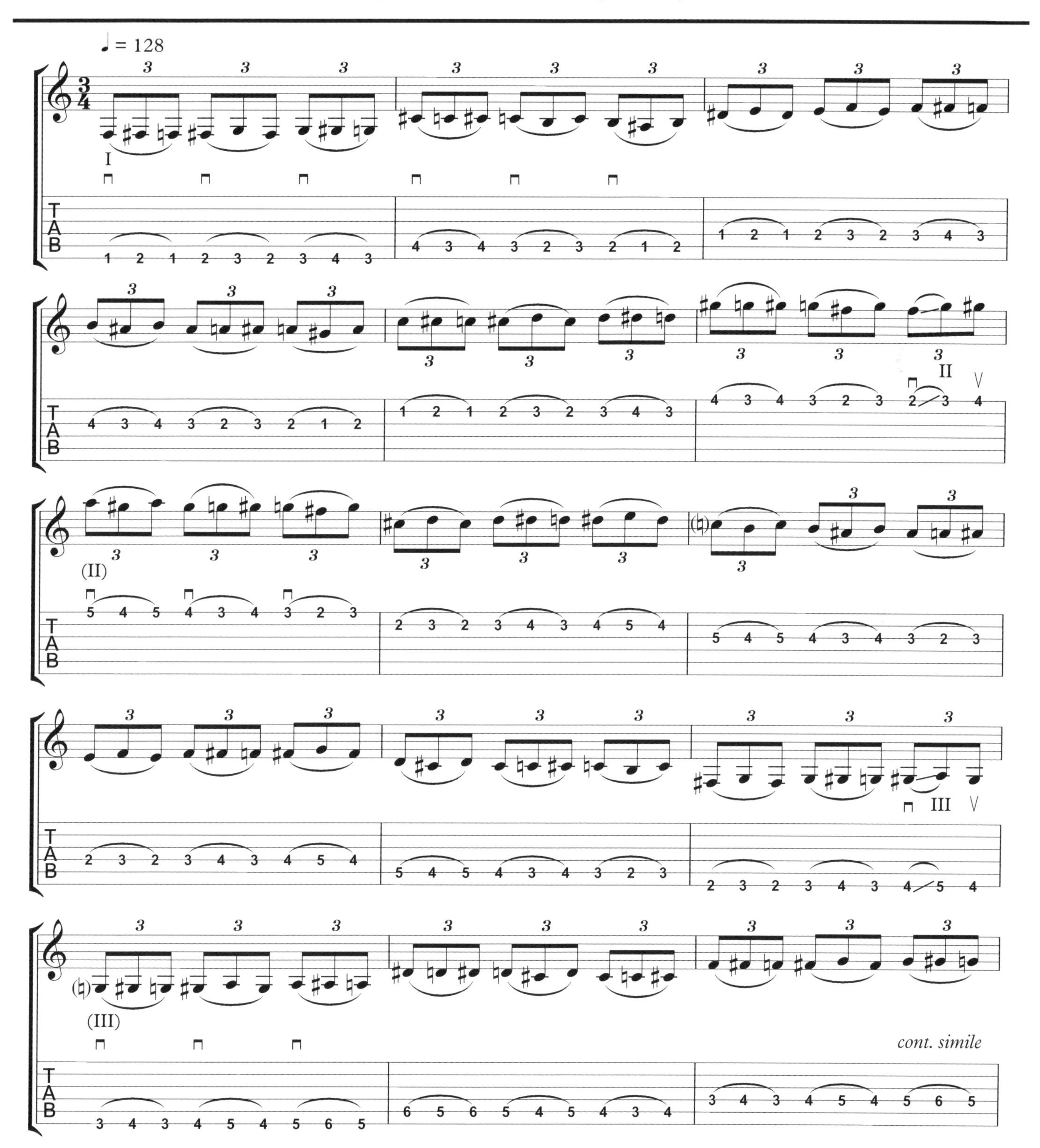

DATE OF COMPLETION: ______________________

LEVEL 3: EXERCISE 76

This exercise will focus on string skipping with eighth note triplets, using the finger pattern 1-2-3-4-2-3. Before completing the pattern in first position, use a legato slide on the high E-string to move into second position and play the reverse finger pattern from the high E-string. This exercise may be played up the entire length of the guitar neck.

DATE OF COMPLETION: ______________________________

LEVEL 3: EXERCISE 77

When using legato slides with sixteenth notes, the note preceding the slide may begin with an upstroke. Pay careful attention to the picking in this exercise, as you will sometimes have to pick two upstrokes in a row – one preceding and one following the slide. Before completing the slide sequence on the high E-string, remove the last downward slide to stay in second position and play the reverse finger pattern from the high E-string. This exercise may be played up the entire length of the guitar neck.

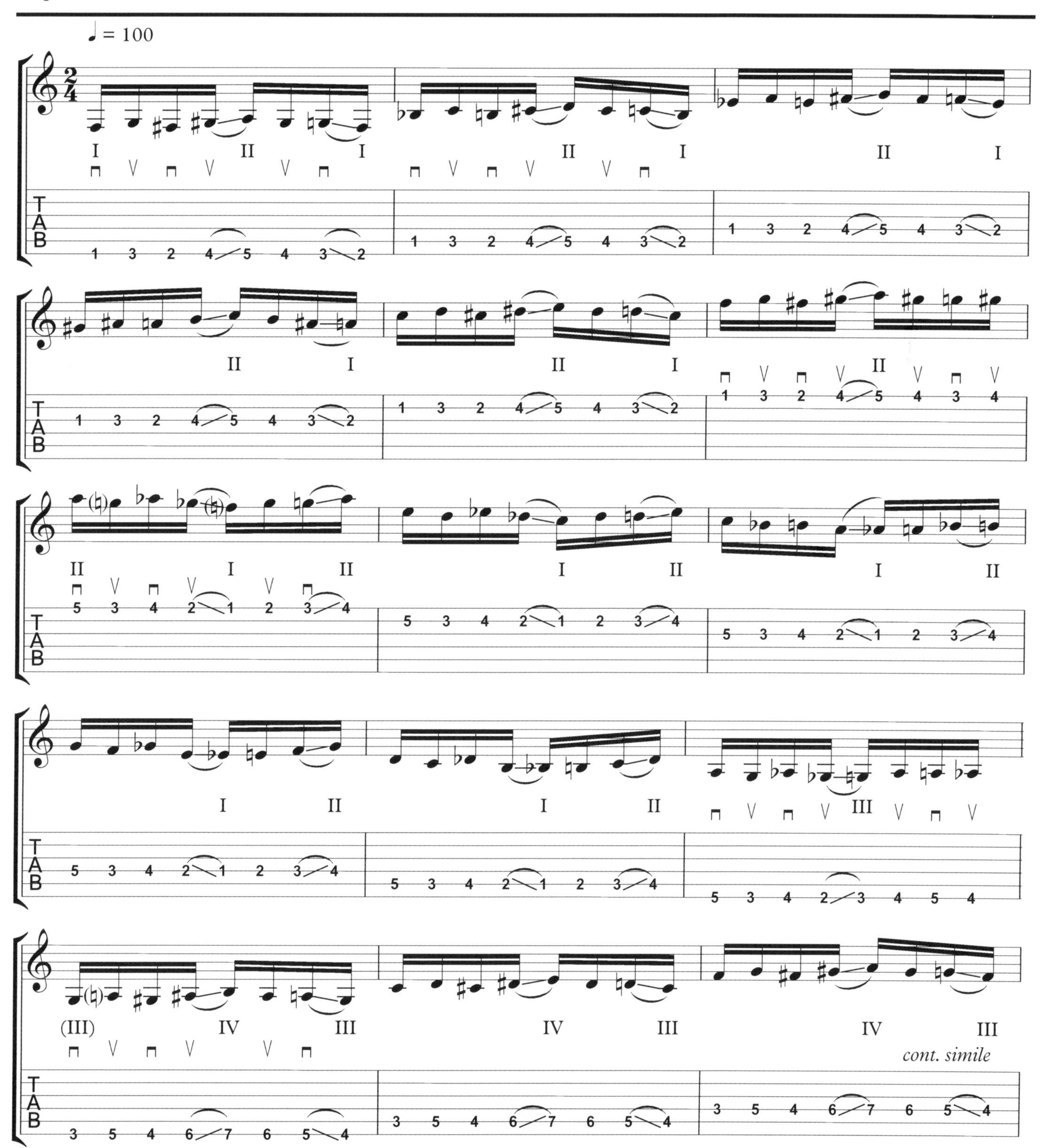

DATE OF COMPLETION: ____________________

LEVEL 3: EXERCISE 78

Similar to legato slides with sixteenth notes, hammer-ons and pull-offs with sixteenth notes may also be preceded by upstrokes. This exercise will include hammer-ons and pull-offs that are preceded by both downstokes and upstrokes. Before completing the pattern in first position, use a legato slide on the high E-string to move into second position and play the reverse finger pattern from the high E-string. This exercise may be played up the entire length of the guitar neck.

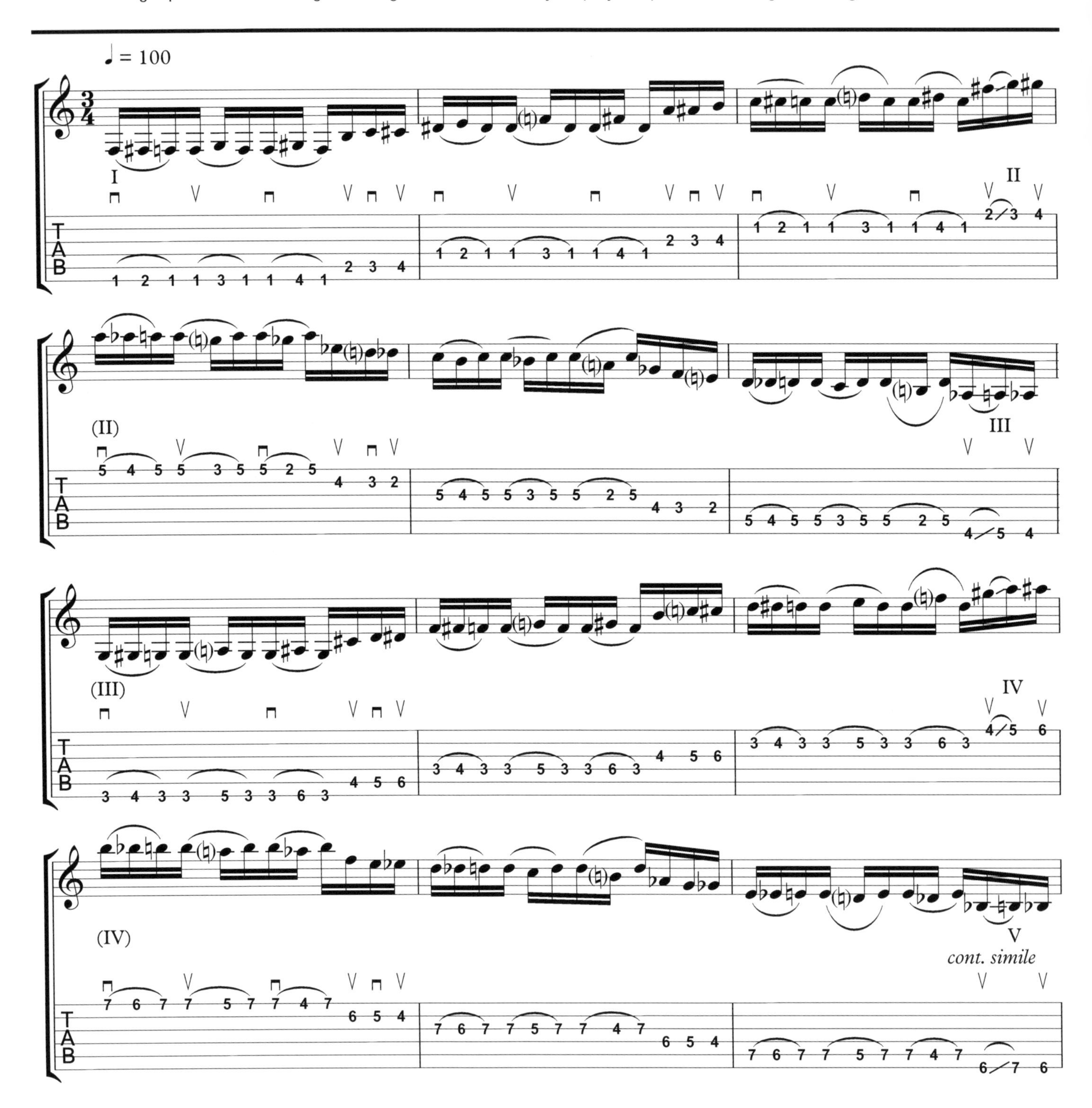

DATE OF COMPLETION: ______________________

LEVEL 3: EXERCISE 79

This exercise will focus on string skipping with sixteenth notes, using the finger patterns 1-3-2-4 and 4-2-3-1. Be sure to roll the 1st and 4th finger when switching to an adjacent higher or lower string. Before completing the finger pattern in first position, use a legato slide on the high E-string to move into second position and play the reverse finger pattern from the high E-string. This exercise may be played up the entire length of the neck.

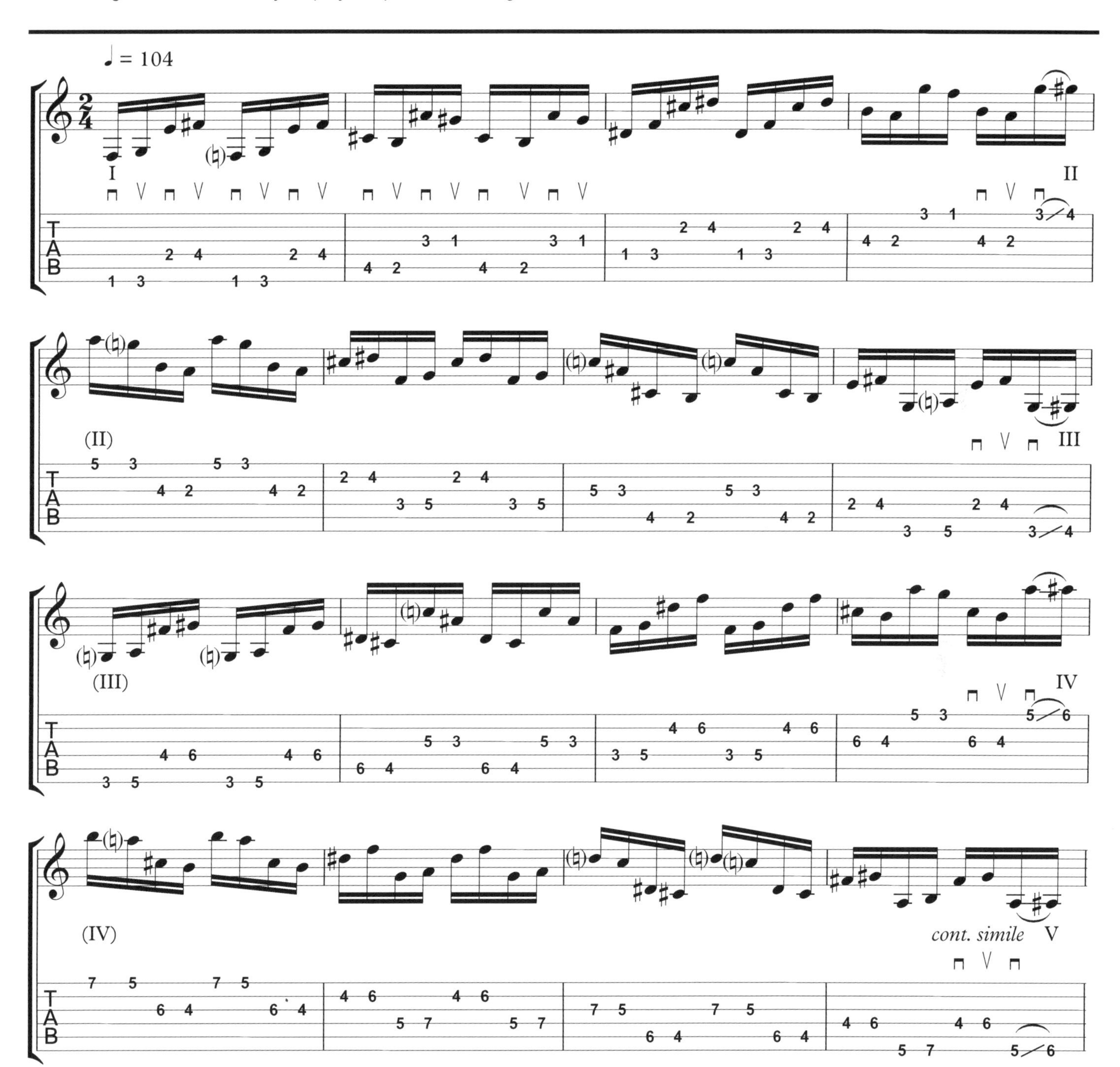

DATE OF COMPLETION: ______________________

BOOKS IN THIS SERIES

LEVEL 1

Coordinate your guitar playing in the most fundamental way by practicing over 20 basic patterns of linear playing, string switching, string skipping, slides, hammer-ons and pull-offs.

LEVEL 2

Increase your abilities with eighth note picking and advanced finger patterns. The development of alternate picking will allow for faster rhythms and even more complex guitar technique exercises.

LEVEL 3

Teach your fingers to react how you want and when you want when playing triplets and sixteenth notes. Plus, the advanced technique exercises will prepare your fingers for any music you need to play.

COMPLETE GUIDE

Over 70 exercises will guide you from the simplest aspects of guitar coordination through the speed studies and techniques of the professionals.

ALSO BY GREG STUDLEY...

A GUITARIST'S GUIDE TO IMPROVISING WITH KNOWLEDGE

(to be released in late 2013)

Finally, an answer to each and every guitarist who has had that moment of simultaneous bliss and confusion when listening to one of their idol players and thinking, "How did they come up with that solo? Will I ever be able to play like that?"

Improvising With Knowledge will show you how to:

· play major and minor pentatonic scale shapes ·

· move these shapes around the neck ·

· improvise over chord progressions by following the chords ·

· create rhythmic and melodic patterns in your solos ·

· incorporate arpeggios that fit each particular chord ·

· and much more! ·

Visit www.improvisingwithknowledge.com
for free videos, downloads and jam tracks.

GREG STUDLEY

Greg Studley has spent years advancing his technique as a professional guitarist and music instructor. In over ten years of teaching, he has worked with students of all ages and skill levels, from those learning the basics to professionals looking to finely tune their musical abilities and understanding. Greg earned his degree in Jazz Performance from Loyola University New Orleans and currently teaches guitar, bass and piano in San Francisco, CA. He also spends time working as a musician in the the Bay Area's studio scene, performing regularly around the western US, and has established the popular website www.improvisingwithknowledge.com for guitar players looking to advance their soloing skills.